PSYCHOLOGICAL ISSUES

VOL. VIII, No. 2 MONOGRAPH 30

PSYCHOANALYTIC RESEARCH:

THREE APPROACHES TO THE EXPERIMENTAL STUDY OF SUBLIMINAL PROCESSES

Edited by
MARTIN MAYMAN

INTERNATIONAL UNIVERSITIES PRESS, INC.
239 Park Avenue South • New York, N.Y. 10003

Library of Congress Cataloguing in Publication Data

PSYCHOANALYTIC RESEARCH.
(Psychological issues, v. 8, no. 2. Monograph 30)
"Presented in abbreviated form at the 1966 annual meeting of the American Psychological Association."
Bibliography: p.
1. Psychoanalysis—Congresses. 2. Psychiatric research—Congresses. 3. Subliminal projection—Congresses. I. Mayman, Martin, ed. II. American Psychological Association. III. Series. [DNLM: 1. Psychoanalysis. 2. Subliminal stimulation. W1 PS572 v. 8 no. 2 1973. XNLM: [WM 460 M469p 1973]]

RC506.P78 616.8'917 73-2848
ISBN 0-8236-4490-1

PSYCHOLOGICAL ISSUES

Subscription per Volume, $15.00
Single Copies of This Number, $5.00

CONTENTS

ACKNOWLEDGMENTS

Chapter 1 is a revised version of "Activation and Measurement of an Early Oral Fantasy: An Exploratory Study," *Journal of the American Psychoanalytic Association,* 15:99–129, 1967, and appears by permission of the editor of the *Journal* and International Universities Press.

In Chapter 3, "Brain Wave Correlates of Subliminal Stimulation, Unconscious Attention, Primary- and Secondary-Process Thinking, and Repressiveness," Figures 1 and 6 first appeared in Shevrin, H., and Fritzler, D. E., "Visual Evoked Response Correlates of Unconscious Mental Processes," *Science,* 161 (July 19):295–298, 1968. Copyright 1968 by the American Association for the Advancement of Science; reproduced by permission. Figure 2 first appeared in Shevrin, H., and Fisher, C., "Changes in the Effects of a Waking Subliminal Stimulus as a Function of Dreaming and Nondreaming Sleep," *Journal of Abnormal Psychology,* 72:362–368, 1967. Copyright 1967 by the American Psychological Association; reproduced by permission. Figures 4 and 5 and Table 1 first appeared in Shevrin, H., and Rennick, P., "Cortical Response to a Tactile Stimulus during Attention, Mental Arithmetic and Free Associations," *Psychophysiology,* 3:381–388, 1967. Copyright 1967 The Williams & Wilkins Co., Baltimore; reproduced by permission. Figure 7 and Table 2 first appeared in Shevrin, H., and Fritzler, D. E., "Brain Response Correlates of Repressiveness," *Psychological Reports,* 23:887–892, 1968; reproduced by permission of the publisher. Figure 8 first appeared in Shevrin, H., Smith, W. H., and Fritzler, D. E., "Repressiveness as a Factor in the Subliminal Activation of Brain and Verbal Responses," *Journal of Nervous and Mental Disease,* 149:261–269, 1969. Copyright 1969 The Williams & Wilkins Co., Baltimore; reproduced by permission.

INTRODUCTION

REFLECTIONS ON PSYCHOANALYTIC RESEARCH

MARTIN MAYMAN

This symposium was presented in abbreviated form at the 1966 annual meeting of the American Psychological Association under the title, "A Psychoanalyst and a Methodologist Look at Two Examples of Psychoanalytic Research." It marked an auspicious occasion: the first time, to my knowledge, that the scientifically purist Division of Experimental Psychology cosponsored a symposium with the avowedly clinical Society for Projective Techniques. The theme of the symposium, however, is not at all novel. It is in fact something of a decennial occurrence, as the attached bibliography attests (see Supplemental Bibliography, p. 126). One might suppose that still another go-around on the feasibility or failings of "psychoanalytic research" could offer little more than a rehash of old issues, any novelty in it coming only from the expressive style or conceptual elegance of the presentations. But it seemed to us several years ago that such reservations might not be justified, for psychoanalytic research in the 1950s and 1960s has taken several new turns. Surely something must have been added to the psychoanalytic scene if a symposium like this one could win the endorsement of the most skeptical, hard-nosed, often anticlinical and antipsychoanalytic group of psychologists in the American Psychological Association.

It is, of course, still fashionable in some academic circles to question the credentials of psychoanalysis when it puts itself forward as a young but nonetheless eminently presentable member of the family of sciences. One of the fictions we have learned to live with is the widely held belief that psychoanalysis falls far short of its claims to status as a science and has, in fact, produced little in the way of an empirical-experimental literature which could extend the growing edge of the science, something every self-respecting science must do to remain viable. Often, the more jaundiced attacks of this sort have condescendingly dismissed Freud's pretensions as a scientist. This judgment, like so many others directed at psychoanalysis, errs out of regrettable unfamiliarity with what Freud actually had to say. His writings provide imposing evidence that Freud was a most incisive and clear-thinking methodologist, capable of turning a very objective and critical eye on the logical structure and veridical cogency of psychoanalytic thought. He may have directed good-natured jibes at methodologists for "forever polishing their glasses and never looking through them," but he himself did not fail to stop on occasion to polish his own methodological glasses. Some of his parenthetical asides have even found their way into textbooks on the philosophy of science. Abraham Kaplan (1964), for example, cites with approval Freud's often-quoted argument against premature formalism or tightness of concept definition in a young, evolving science:

> We have often heard it maintained that sciences should be built up on clear and sharply defined basic concepts. In actual fact no science, not even the most exact, begins with such definitions. The true beginning of scientific activity consists rather in describing phenomena and then in proceeding to group, classify and correlate them. Even at the stage of description it is not possible to avoid applying certain abstract ideas to the material in hand, ideas derived from somewhere or other but certainly not from the new observations alone. . . . The basic concepts of the science . . . must at first necessarily possess some degree of indefiniteness; there can be no question of any clear delimitation of their content. So long as they remain in this condition, we come to an understanding about their meaning by making repeated references to the material of observation from which they appear to have been derived, but upon which, in fact, they have been imposed. Thus, strictly speaking, they are in the nature of conventions—although everything depends on their not being arbitrarily chosen but determined by their having significant relations to the empirical material, relations that we seem to

sense before we can clearly recognize and demonstrate them. It is only after more thorough investigation of the field of observation that we are able to formulate its basic scientific concepts with increased precision, and progressively so to modify them that they become serviceable and consistent over a wide area. Then, indeed, the time may have come to confine them in definitions. The advance of knowledge, however, does not tolerate any rigidity even in definitions. Physics furnishes an excellent illustration of the way in which even 'basic concepts' that have been established in the form of definitions are constantly being altered in their content [Freud, 1915a, p. 117].

This was an assertion Freud returned to over and over again, with equal incisiveness and assurance:

> Psycho-analysis is not, like philosophies, a system starting out from a few sharply defined basic concepts, seeking to grasp the whole universe with the help of these and, once it is completed, having no room for fresh discoveries or better understanding. On the contrary, it keeps close to the facts in its field of study, seeks to solve the immediate problems of observation, gropes its way forward by the help of experience, is always incomplete and always ready to correct or modify its theories. There is no incongruity (any more than in the case of physics or chemistry) if its most general concepts lack clarity and if its postulates are provisional; it leaves their more precise definition to the results of future work [Freud, 1923, pp. 253–254].

> . . . we have no other aim but that of translating into theory the results of observation, and we deny that there is any obligation on us to achieve at our very first attempt a well-rounded theory which will commend itself by its simplicity. We shall defend the complications of our theory so long as we find that they meet the results of observation, and we shall not abandon our expectations of being led in the end by those very complications to the discovery of a state of affairs which, while simple in itself, can account for all the complications of reality [Freud, 1915b, p. 190].

One could, if one wished, build an entire monograph around the many and varied observations Freud advanced concerning psychoanalytic epistemology.

Freud repeatedly resisted the pull of philosophy in favor of an empirical science, but at the same time had no taste at all for the drudgery of experimental proofs. Out of the vast experimental literature that accumulated in the half century of his active professional life, only three investigators who used experimental or naturalistic approaches other than psychoanalysis drew favorable comment from him—Charcot, for his prepsychoanalytic studies of hypnosis, and Varendonck and Pötzl, about whom more will be said shortly. No, Freud's heart lay elsewhere than with experiment; he was given over to the pleasures of discovery. The more subdued satisfaction of going over old ground to confirm what had already been learned held little appeal for him. His life was spent in the creative pursuit of hypothesis finding, not the pedestrian pursuit of hypothesis testing. And the world is much the better for it. Methodologists sometimes lose sight of the fact that it is discovery, not research, that is the life blood of a science. Colby put it well when he said:

> Scientific inquiry begins with a problem and bright-idea hypotheses about it. To see a problem, to feel it is worth solving, and to search, guided by hypotheses, for the hidden explanatory pattern constitutes the essence of discovery. Those procedural rules which we term "scientific methods" do not create discoveries; they can only increase the probability that a discovery is true [1960, p. 109].

Nonetheless, the work of hypothesis testing, the work of research, must be done, and if not by Freud, then by those who come after him. That work has been attempted, sometimes for better, sometimes for worse. Perhaps the best overview of this field is provided by Hilgard, Kubie, and Pumpian-Mindlin in their book, *Psychoanalysis as Science* (Pumpian-Mindlin, 1952). They touch on most of the important tributaries which have fed into a 50-year flow of psychoanalytic and quasi-psychoanalytic research which, almost without exception, has been interesting but, also almost without exception, disappointing in its theoretical yield.

That is the only conclusion one can draw from an uninterrupted series of experiments on hypnotic induction of psychoanalytic phenomena. This line of research dates back to the early work by Schrötter (1911), Roffenstein (1924), and Nachmansohn (1925) on dream symbolism and the dream work. It was picked up in the 1930s and subsequently in a long series of publications by Milton Erickson (1939) and others. But for all of its initial promise, experimentation with hypnosis has been, on balance. disappointing. Except for the work of Gill and Brenman (1959), it has added little to our knowledge of thought processes in general or dream processes in particular. Hypnosis has yet to become a tool which does more than merely duplicate observations which psychoanalysis has already made without its help.

The 1930s and 1940s saw the parallel emergence of a quite different way of going about creating laboratory analogues of psychoanalytic phenomena—the induction of conflicts and defense not only in human beings but in infrahuman creatures as well (Miller, 1948; Sears, 1943, 1944; Rosenzweig and Mason, 1934; Rosenzweig, 1937). But with rare exceptions (Keet, 1948) these studies, like the studies using hypnosis, were so designed that, at best, they could do no more than duplicate psychoanalytic knowledge; they could not extend it. Except for some very superficial similarities, they had little bearing on psychoanalysis proper.

More convincing in its relevance to psychoanalysis was a quite different line of research which set about testing predictions drawn from psychoanalytic characterology. The animal studies by Levy (1934, 1952), Hunt (1941), and others (Beach and Jaynes, 1954); similar predictions with human subjects by Goldman (1948) and Blum (1949); studies of psychosexual correlates of clinical psychopathology (Alexander and Menninger, 1936; Beech, 1959; Schmidt and Brown, 1965); and psychosexual correlates of other aspects of character structure (Rosenwald, 1972; Rosenwald et al., 1966; V. G. Schlesinger, 1963)—all these studies have successfully supported many of the generalizations arrived at by psychoanalysis from individual case studies.

One could cite other approaches which have become important new developments in the concerted effort to duplicate in the laboratory the discoveries of psychoanalysis, in order to sharpen, clarify, and extend psychoanalytic formulations. Psychological testing became, in the hands of its most brilliant innovators—

Murray, Rorschach, Rapaport–the operational right arm of psychoanalytic ego psychology.

Nor should one overlook the many nonexperimental ventures into theory testing which were launched in the 1940s and 1950s. Systematic study of the treatment hour (Shakow, 1960; Gill et al., 1968; Simon, 1970), of therapy process and outcome (A. Freud, 1959; Wallerstein et al., 1956; Kernberg et al., 1972), of children at home and in nurseries, clinics, and hospitals (Spitz, 1945, 1946; Spitz and Wolf, 1946a, 1946b; Benjamin, 1950; Escalona, 1952, 1968; Wolff, 1963, 1964; Fraiberg and collaborators, 1964, 1966), have provided new impetus to a long-overdue housecleaning and refurbishing of psychoanalytic postulates and propositions (Sandler, 1962a, 1962b; Nagera et al., 1969). The drawback of some of these studies, especially those which gather complete audio and video tape recordings of psychoanalytic sessions, is the mountain of raw data with which they inundate the investigators. Perhaps the ultimate usefulness of such research awaits the application of computer technology along lines suggested by Jaffe (1963) and more recently by Dahl and Spence (Simon, 1970). But these studies are essentially naturalistic in their approach, and fall outside the scope of psychoanalytic experimentation, essential as they may eventually prove to be. This very sketchy survey concerns itself rather with *experimental* contributions to psychoanalytic theory. Concerning these, it is regrettably still the case that

> . . . the existing surveys [of this experimental literature]–Sears (1943), Rapaport (1943), Hilgard (1952)–are either specialized or incomplete. A careful analytic survey of the pertinent experimental literature would be a formidable undertaking: the amount of literature on research purporting to be related and on research actually related to psychoanalytic theory is immense. Yet such a survey is urgently needed. It would be of most use if it were to center neither on the design of the experiments nor on their results, but rather on the relation of the methods used to the theory [Rapaport, 1959a, p. 110].

If any one conclusion can be drawn from most of the studies

which make up the history of "psychoanalytic" experimentation, it is unfortunately that reached by Kubie:

> Many of these laboratory charades are pedestrian and limited demonstrations of things which have been proved over and over again in real life. This is another reason why men who are going to experiment in this field should first become sophisticated as to what nature itself can tell them. Experimental facilities should not be wasted on issues which are already clearly proved, and to which human bias alone continues to blind us. The experimentalist should rather take up where the naturalist leaves off. He may ask the naturalist to guide him on a field trip so that he can satisfy himself concerning the observations which the naturalist has made and has brought to him for investigation. It is not his duty or responsibility, however, to prove in the laboratory the existence of data which the naturalist reports to him. Much controversy about the empirical data of analysis has arisen because people have refused to look at facts which are clearly observable in the analytic situation. These parallel the controversies which arose over Van Leuwenhock's microscope among men who had never used it yet who refused to believe in the reality of what he reported. Similarly there are many who have refused to look through the microscope of analysis, or to create a relationship with a child or an adult which would make it possible for that child or adult to express his fantasies undistorted by conscious restrictions. Such self-imposed blindness is usually expressed in terms of critical skepticism and as a demand for experimental proofs where simple objective observation would make this superfluous [1952, p. 64].

Few experimental studies can, in retrospect, be said to have contributed significantly to the formulation of psychoanalytic propositions, to the structure of psychoanalytic theory, or to the body of psychoanalytic findings.

It is against the backdrop of 50 years of laboratory research into psychoanalytic phenomena that the work of Spence, Luborsky, and Shevrin reported in the present volume should be viewed. The three do not stand outside psychoanalysis looking in, trying to see if there may be something to the theory after all. They are all trained, committed, and practicing psychoanalysts bent on pushing the theory beyond its present limits; each tries to carry the theory forward to an uncovering of new data. All three explore the possibilities inherent in new methods which supplement rather than supplant the original and still primary method of data gathering in psychoanalysis. They come full circle and pick up where Varendonck (1921) and Pötzl (1917) left off fully 50 years ago. This is paradoxical, because the leading reviews of this experimental literature in psychoanalysis have nothing to say about the contributions of Varendonck and Pötzl. It was Varendonck who first hit upon a quasi-psychoanalytic method for studying daydreams while he was in the trenches during the First World War. His research method was not unlike that used by Silberer (1909) and more recently by Rapaport (1951b, 1957) to study preconscious thought processes. Varendonck identified the definitive attributes of daydreams, taking a first but large step toward differentiating the many grades of cognition which fall between the so-called "secondary process' and "primary process" modes of thought (Rapaport, 1957; Klein, 1959; Gill, 1967; Holt, 1967). He used data gathered in an "experiment of nature," but as Kubie points out, these ready-made phenomena which present themselves without the artificial mediation of the experimental laboratory are no less scientific than laboratory research if they are treated carefully, objectively, and systematically. This method of research is a sorely neglected one; its potential is amply demonstrated again in the studies Luborsky reports upon in this monograph.

Pötzl (1917), at almost the same time, involved himself in another aspect of the same problem, the manner in which a day residue impinges on the psyche, is registered and elaborated upon in the unconscious, and is eventually retrieved by consciousness in the form of a dream image rather than a consciously evoked (or evocable) memory. Pötzl came up with the remarkable finding that it is precisely those elements of the stimulus of which the person was least aware originally that are most likely to find their way into the manifest content of dreams. This conclusion not only confirmed but went beyond what Freud had to say about the use of day residues in the dream work. In the next 30 years Pötzl's discovery was followed up only twice, by Allers and Teler (1924) and Malamud and Lindner (1931). Not until the 1950s did this avenue of research gain the attention it deserved, largely through the efforts of Fisher (1954, 1956, 1965), Luborsky and Shevrin (1956), Shevrin and Luborsky (1958), and Klein (1959). The studies reported by Spence and Shevrin in this monograph developed largely out of this important current of research.

Each of the research contributions to this volume is, in the final analysis, part of a program of research which was first proposed by Freud in his papers on metapsychology. Almost from its inception, psychoanalysis has looked forward to the day when it would know a good deal more about the interrelations between the various "systems of the mind":

> It would put an end to all misunderstandings if, from now on, in describing the various kinds of psychical acts we were to disregard the question of whether they were conscious or unconscious, and were to classify and correlate them . . . according to their composition and according to which of the hierarchy of psychical systems they belong to [Freud, 1915b, p. 172].

Some 45 years later Klein was able to summarize a body of research which showed conclusively that this aim of Freud's was no vain hope:

> Proper and precise use of the terms awareness and of consciousness will alert us to the productive possibilities of the options which Freud won by giving up certain popular connotations of the term consciousness. Thus in speaking of registrations without awareness instead of preconscious perception, we are alerted to (a) the superordinate organization–the state of consciousness–in which such registrations occur; (b) the elaborations to which they are subject in primary or secondary process terms; and (c) the controlling organizations which shape their emergence in different forms of experience, e.g., as images or perceptions [Klein, 1959, p. 31].

Spence, Luborsky, and Shevrin have continued this work, employing, as did Klein, the methods of experimental research for this purpose. In the first three chapters we shall hear reports of three examples of psychoanalytic research. Luborsky shows how an observation in the consulting room led to a hypothesis, which in turn led to a form of experimental test and to an important new paradigm of psychoanalytic research. This paper was one of the first of a series on the application of this very promising method to the systematic research analysis of minute occurrences in the treatment hour (Luborsky, 1953, 1967; Luborsky and Auerbach, 1969). Spence, too, started with a clinical observation, went on to formulate a psychoanalytic reconstruction of processes which could account for that observation, and then designed an experimental laboratory test of his hypotheses. Shevrin demonstrates the potential fruitfulness of imaginative research technology which can give access to an entirely new body of data relevant to some of the issues of psychoanalytic psychology. All three attempt to examine ego processes at a level of registration and response where some exquisitely subtle influences upon the ego can be isolated from the informational "noise" which normally drowns out such observations. Each investigator has in his own way tried to forge new instruments with the help of which he can draw closer to processes which are of central interest to psychoanalysis proper. Holzman and Meehl follow with presentations of their views on the philosophical and practical problems involved in developing psychoanalytically relevant hypotheses into methodologically sound research.

Klein's concluding thoughts 10 years ago are a fitting introduction to these studies:

> Obviously much more work is needed to exploit the potential of the psychoanalytic concept of consciousness for dealing with one of the central problems of psychology—the range of human sensibility to meaning. Academic psychology has tried off and on through the years to slough off the problems of consciousness and unconsciousness, but the ghosts have lived on. Through the momentum provided by the structural concepts of current psychoanalytic theory and by recent advances in observational techniques, there is real possibility that the ghosts will become at last very corporeal and manageable realities in the experimental laboratory [1959, p. 32].

1

ACTIVATION AND ASSESSMENT OF AN EARLY ORAL FANTASY: AN EXPLORATORY STUDY

DONALD P. SPENCE
CAROL M. GORDON

A concern with fantasy in its conscious, preconscious, and unconscious manifestations has been growing in recent years; since 1960, papers on the subject by Beres (1962), Arlow (1969), Sandler and Nagera (1963), and the proceedings of an international Symposium on Fantasy (1964) have appeared. Consensus on what is meant by fantasy seems to vary with its distance from awareness, being fairly good with respect to conscious fantasy, fair with respect to preconscious fantasy, and almost lacking so far as unconscious fantasy is concerned. This is not surprising: preconscious and unconscious fantasies are inferred from their derivatives, and the inferences can be checked only when the fantasy itself comes into awareness. Frequently that never happens, and the investigator is left with a speculation which, however reasonable, can never be directly tested. Furthermore, there is reason to wonder whether the fantasy, when it does emerge, is identical with the fantasy that gave rise to the derivatives. Kohut, for example, questions "the correctness of the assumption that the observed fantasy products from the Unconscious . . . are identical with the unobserved fantasies; . . . we seem inclined to surmise that they change in the process of becoming observable" (1964, p. 200).

Up to several years ago, the difficulty in getting exact reconstructions does not seem to have attracted much concern. Recently, however, Beres and Sandler and Nagera picked up

A longer version of this chapter appeared in the *Journal of the American Psychoanalytic Association,* 15:99-129, 1967.

Freud's original assertion that a preconscious fantasy can be very highly organized, even though it is outside of awareness; thus an accurate reconstruction becomes of interest because an organized preconscious fantasy seems to be an outstanding exception to the general rule that the level of organization of a thought is a function of the degree to which it is conscious.

Not only can a fantasy be highly organized even though it is not in awareness; one might even take the position that a fantasy can be highly organized *because* it lies outside of awareness. This apparent paradox stems from the fact that many fantasies are based on wishes formed at an early stage of development and not easily tolerated by the adult ego. They become adaptively distorted when admitted into consciousness, and as a result may appear incoherent, formless, vague, and rambling. The transformation parallels the transformation from latent to manifest dream; the manifest dream typically appears to be unorganized and nonsensical, although it stems from a highly organized dream thought.

In sum, we might speculate that one of the important characteristics of a fantasy is its high degree of organization; that this organization is protected by its position outside of awareness; and that any attempt to study the fantasy and assess its form and content must be carried out on the fantasy in its natural state. Clearly an approach which depends on inferences from projective material or derivatives during treatment is not altogether satisfactory, because the inferences cannot easily be checked, because the content may change as it emerges into awareness, and because the critical question concerns the fantasy itself and not its offshoots.

In the usual procedure for assessing a fantasy, we look for its influence on conscious thought, but we have no control over the changes that may take place in a fantasy as it comes into awareness. One way to reduce this distortion is to use a sensing instrument that is also outside of awareness, enabling us to assess the fantasy in its natural state. Here is where a subliminal stimulus may be useful: it too is outside of awareness and may serve as a mediating instrument, allowing us to assess the fantasy before it becomes distorted.

Our experimental procedure was modeled on an incident that

occurred during analytic treatment of a patient of the senior author's in whom a severe rejection caused a craving for food and cigarettes. We set up a situation in which some subjects were made to feel rejected, both directly and indirectly. Shipley and Veroff (1952) have shown that a similar kind of rejection can arouse a wish for affiliation, reflected in TAT stories–a conscious thought product. We would expect rejection to have effects extending much further outside of awareness and possibly to arouse an oral fantasy, especially if the subjects tended to equate food and affection, as did the analytic patient.

ASSESSMENT OF THE FANTASY

Suppose that an oral fantasy is aroused by our procedure, and suppose (because we are working with a normal population) that it is descriptively unconscious. It might show itself in various derivatives, and these would be highly variable and hard to assess because they would be based on individual defensive reactions. Some would be idiosyncratically distorted; others would be neutralized and so devoid of obvious significance that their emergence would tell us nothing about the underlying fantasy.

Now suppose that we expose the subliminal stimulus "milk" to subjects immediately after the fantasy is aroused. Previous studies have shown that a subliminal stimulus will reinforce certain associated ideas–if we show a subject the word "cheese," for example, it helps him to notice and recall the word "mouse" in a list of words read aloud. Another study by Cofer (1962) has shown that–on the conscious level–the context of a stimulus word is important in determining what associates it will arouse. The word "dress," for example, produces associations of cloth, girl, etc., whereas "frayed dress" produces associations of old, torn, ragged, and accident. We might expect that the word "milk" shown subliminally would activate or mesh with an infantile set. This is merely restating, in somewhat more operational language, what we expect of a day residue: it is ambiguous, and the associates it produces in a dream are partly determined by the simultaneously aroused infantile wish.

In subjects to whom the subliminal stimulus was exposed, we would look for words linked to both milk and the infantile fantasy, such as breast, warm, mouth, etc. In what form would they emerge? In a clinical setting, derivatives frequently appear as intrusions into the patient's associations—a slip of the tongue, for example, or a peculiar choice of words, or undue emphasis on a commonplace phrase. Suppose the experimental subject is asked to learn a list of words. We know from experience that other words (importations) will be recalled in addition to those actually on the list, and that a derivative might appear as such an error. Consequently, we might hypothesize that following the subliminal stimulus, we would find, in the subjects who felt rejected, more importations related jointly to milk and the theme of an infantile oral fantasy.

Now suppose that an infantile fantasy has been aroused by rejection, but that recall is *not* preceded by a mediating subliminal stimulus. As we have already mentioned, derivatives of the fantasy would very likely be idiosyncratically distorted by each subject's conscious concerns. The total group effect would seem to be randomly organized, and the conclusion would follow that no fantasy had been aroused. Thus, quite different inferences would be drawn about the underlying fantasy in the second condition (no subliminal stimulus) compared to the first, in which a subliminal stimulus was presented, and one might conclude either that there was no underlying fantasy, or that it was vague, undifferentiated, and poorly organized. The hypothesis that fantasies have a specific preconscious organization would be rejected because of the nature of the experimental design.

Not only do fantasies show themselves in derivatives; clinical experience tells us that they also influence conscious recall. A patient may notice certain street signs on the way to an hour, and from his selection we may be able to reconstruct an underlying fantasy. We can duplicate this event experimentally by presenting a subject with two sets of words to learn, and looking for a selective effect on recall brought about by the fantasy. Suppose the subjects are asked to learn two subsets of milk associates—one related to the infantile nursing situation and containing the words warm, mother, suck, etc., and the other more socialized, containing the words glass, dairy, butter, etc. If the infantile fantasy has been aroused, we would expect the first set of milk associates to be better recalled than the second, on the assumption that the fantasy has biased the associative network.

Now suppose an infantile fantasy has been aroused but that the list of words to be learned is presented without a mediating subliminal stimulus. One possible result is that the infantile fantasy would not be admissible to consciousness and its derivatives would be modified in line with reality: our second set of associates—words like glass, dairy, and butter—would be stressed in recall, and instead of a fantasy about the original nursing situation we would see one related to eating or drinking in a more everyday context. We might then assume that the original fantasy was much less infantile than was actually the case, and once again the organization hypothesis would be rejected because of the experimental design.

PROCEDURE

AROUSAL OF THE ORAL FANTASY

The rejection procedure was modeled on an experimental procedure used by Shipley and Veroff (1952). The subjects (undergraduates) were told that we were studying how people form friendships at first sight; to that end, each person was asked to stand and give his name. While he was standing, the rest of the class was told to rate him on a 7-point scale on how much they would like to have him as a friend. After all subjects had been rated, each person was asked to list the names of the five people he would be most likely to choose for friends.

The stress generated by this exposure could be seen in two ways: subjects frequently announced their names in a mumble, possibly audible to their immediate neighbors but not to the class at large; and they typically stood for only a brief period and then immediately sat down. Both of these actions would tend to prevent them from being identified and thus might reduce the risk of their being rated unfavorably.

After all students had been rated (the rating was done anonymously to encourage a free expression of feelings), we collected all the scores and pretended to look through them for popular and unpopular students. After 5 to 10 minutes had elapsed, we read off the names of half the class who had, we said, been selected by a majority as persons they would most like to have as friends. This group would take part in the main experiment (they will be called the "accepted subjects"). The others were told that they would not be used in the main study and that we would ask them to close their eyes when the time came (they will be called the "rejected subjects"). It will be noted that we added our rejection as experimenters to the rejection apparently handed them by their peers. As a final touch, we gave each of the rejected subjects a bluebook that was lacking its front cover; the accepted subjects, on the other hand, received an intact book.

The two groups did not, in fact, differ in popularity, despite our statements: they had been randomly divided in advance, and a check of the ratings showed that subjects in both groups had been chosen by their peers about an equal number of times as one of the most liked students.

Did the experimental manipulation really make subjects feel rejected? To investigate this question we asked all subjects to write stories to three TAT cards—Nos. 6BM, 14, and 20—and later scored the stories for mention of rejection, loneliness, physical departure, and other related themes. These categories were taken from Shipley and Veroff (1952), who found that a somewhat similar kind of rejection brought about an increase in stories related to these themes. After the stories, for a second check on the procedure, each subject rated himself for feelings of rejection on a 7-point scale which ranged from "Very rejected" to "Very accepted."

INDIVIDUAL DIFFERENCES

It is evident that not all persons will respond to rejection with a strong oral fantasy. We assumed, however, that our population of subjects would include a number who tended to use food as a substitute for affection, and that in these subjects a loss of affection (rejection) would be particularly likely to activate thoughts and fantasies related to food. We therefore constructed a questionnaire designed to identify highly oral subjects. It consisted of 12 items (e.g., "When I'm feeling blue I try to find something to eat"; "If my food is cold I feel lonely and down in the dumps"), each of which could be answered "Always," "Frequently," "Occasionally," or "Never," and scored 3, 2, 1, and 0 respectively. A high score indicated that the subject was aware of using food as a substitute for affection. High-scoring subjects (above the median) will be called "high oral," and low-scoring subjects "low oral." To prevent the subjects from guessing the central pupose of the experiment, the questionnaire was administered some weeks after the main study.

SUBLIMINAL STIMULUS—THE SENSING INSTRUMENT

If our rationale is correct, an oral fantasy had now been aroused in the rejected subjects, particularly in those who were classified as high oral. We would not assume that such a fantasy, even in our high oral subjects, would be easily admitted to consciousness because of the controlling functions of the ego which guard against such regressive material. To bypass these controlling functions, we exposed the subliminal stimulus "milk," which would, we assumed, be influenced by the undistorted fantasy. As a result of this influence, the stimulus would take on regressive connotations and heighten the recall and importation of infantile associates.

The subliminal stimulus "milk" was flashed five times at 1/150 sec. at low illumination, followed by a clearly visible list of 30 words. Subjects were asked to watch carefully and recall as many words as possible. On the assumption that rejection would arouse a repressed oral fantasy, we selected a cluster of eight words related to the infantile feeding situation (e.g., suck, warm, mother). We added an eight-word cluster of conceptual associates (dairy, glass, butter, etc.) and a control cluster consisting of words related to the word "whistle" to reduce the saturation of food-related words in the list. The three clusters were roughly matched for frequency of occurrence in the written language (Thorndike and Lorge, 1944) and randomly arranged in the list. Since the first and last words on a list are most often recalled, we added three buffer words at the start and three at the end of the list which were not counted in the scoring. The complete list is shown in Figure 1.

Three classes of undergraduates were tested. Two were exposed to the subliminal stimulus in the manner just described. The third (control group) was given the standard rejection and

Infantile Cluster	*Conceptual Cluster*	*Control Cluster*
baby	thirst	game
formula	butter	ring
suck	white	watch
cry	drink	speech
warm	dairy	low
mother	glass	ear
swallow	cold	pierce
sleep	cream	signal

FIGURE 1. Recall list. Complete recall list: comb, paper, road, baby, thirst, game, formula, butter, ring, suck, white, watch, cry, drink, speech, warm, dairy, low, mother, glass, ear, swallow, cold, pierce, sleep, cream, signal, book, porch, idea (first and last three words are buffers).

acceptance procedure and then exposed to a blank slide, followed by the same recall list with the same instructions. The final design, therefore, consists of four subgroups: rejected with subliminal stimulus, rejected with blank slide, accepted with subliminal stimulus, and accepted with blank slide. Our hypothesis was that the infantile fantasy would be aroused in the rejected group, and most clearly reflected in recall when its effect was mediated by the subliminal stimulus. The subliminal-rejected group should show the most effect in general.

After the experiment each subgroup was further divided according to our oral questionnaire. For this purpose we divided our subjects at the median and, as chance would have it, the highs and lows were about equally distributed over the four cells. The final design therefore consists of eight cells.

At the end of the experiment we gave a full explanation of the procedure and explained in some detail how the two groups of rejected and accepted subjects had been selected. We made it clear that the subjects had been placed into the groups at random, that placement had nothing to do with personality characteristics, and that the selection had been made well in advance of the experiment. To confirm this last point we showed a typewritten sheet containing two columns of names, which obviously could not have been made up during the experiment.

RESULTS

EFFECT OF REJECTION

The first question to be considered is, did the experimental rejection produce the desired effect? Let us examine the two check measures. The average self-rating of rejected subjects was closer to the rejected (low) end of the rating scale than was the self-rating of the accepted subjects; the averages were 4.67 and 5.12 respectively, and the difference between the groups approaches significance ($X^2 = 3.34$, $.05 < p < .10$). Thus the experimental rejection did affect the self-rating in the expected direction. On the second measure, the TAT, the number of rejection themes was greater among rejected than accepted subjects, but the difference was not significant. In sum, we have some basis for concluding that the experimental manipulation had an effect in the expected direction.

IMPORTATIONS IN RECALL

The nature of the fantasy aroused by the rejection now becomes our concern. We have hypothesized that it is an oral fantasy and that it should influence importations into the recall list: their content should be related to the oral fantasy. Furthermore, we should find such importations primarily in the rejected-subliminal condition because (a) only in the rejected condition should an oral fantasy be aroused; and (b) only in the rejected-subliminal condition would derivatives of the fantasy be mediated by the subliminal stimulus and appear in awareness more or less without distortion.

Among the imported (falsely remembered) words we found two kinds of oral derivatives: a regressive set that seemed associated with a possible oral fantasy and that included the words milk, bottle, mouth, nipple, smell, and taste, and a more ordinary set, related to food and drink, that included the words bread, eat, food, pea, smoke, and water. We analyzed the two sets separately.

The main findings for the regressive oral importations are shown in Figure 2. Importation of regressive oral words is much

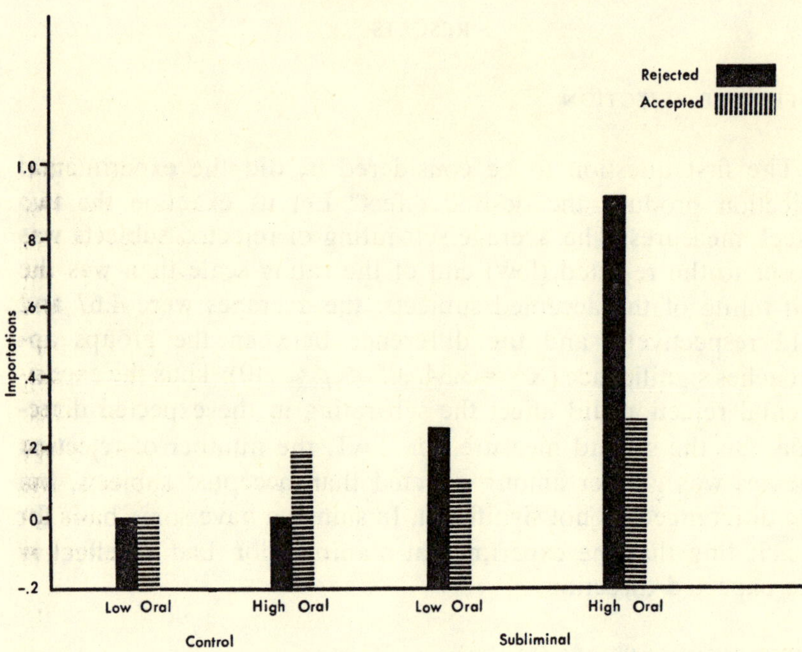

FIGURE 2. Average importation of regressive oral words as a function of experimental rejection, subliminal stimulus, and level of orality.

more frequent in the rejected-subliminal group than in any of the other conditions: more regressive oral words are imported when rejection is followed by a subliminal stimulus than with rejection alone. Second, regressive oral words are not generated by the stimulus unless it is preceded by rejection. Thus a certain kind of fantasy has to be aroused before the subliminal stimulus "milk" generates regressive associates. Third, the control subjects —those who did not see the subliminal stimulus—do not import even one regressive oral word. We would expect more defensive elaboration in this condition; it is possible that some of the non-oral importations were actually derivatives of an oral fantasy, but so defensively distorted as to be unrecognizable. The subliminal stimulus prevents some of these distortions and makes it possible to get a clearer picture of the fantasy in its unconscious state.

Finally, the high oral subjects are most likely to show the main effect. They are the subjects who, on the questionnaire, said that

TABLE 1
ANALYSIS OF VARIANCE OF IMPORTATIONS OF REGRESSIVE ORAL WORDS

Source	*SS*	*df*	*MS*	*F*
Stimulus (A)	1.88	1	1.88	11.32**
Orality (B)	.94	1	.94	5.66*
Rejection (C)	.39	1	.39	2.35
A x B	.31	1	.31	1.87
A x C	1.09	1	1.09	6.57*
B x C	.08	1	.08	<1
A x B x C	.55	1	.55	3.31
Error	11.11	67	.17	

Note: Method given in Winer (1962, p. 243) for unequal cell frequencies.
* $p < .025$
** $p < .005$

they use food as a substitute for affection; they are the ones who imported the highest number of regressive oral words in the rejected-subliminal condition. The low oral subjects in this condition, although second highest of all the groups, imported appreciably fewer such words. Note, however, that when the subliminal stimulus was not presented, neither high nor low oral rejected subjects imported any regressive oral words. In other words, the mediating stimulus is needed despite a favorable personality pattern.

The differences shown in Figure 2 were tested by a three-way analysis of variance (see Table 1). The analysis shows a main stimulus effect; an effect from orality; and an interaction between stimulus and rejection. This last finding is shown by the fact that in the *subliminal* condition all rejected subjects score higher on importations than do accepted subjects, whereas in the *control* condition all rejected subjects are either equal to, or score below, all accepted subjects.

Now consider the second set of importations–the words bread, eat, food, pea, smoke, and water–shown in Figure 3. It is clear that the amount of importation is essentially the same in all conditions. None of the main differences is significantly different from chance (as tested by a second three-variable analysis of variance). These findings suggest that these particular food importations are produced by something common to all conditions –possibly the word list itself–and not by an underlying fantasy, because they are no more frequent in the rejected than in the ac-

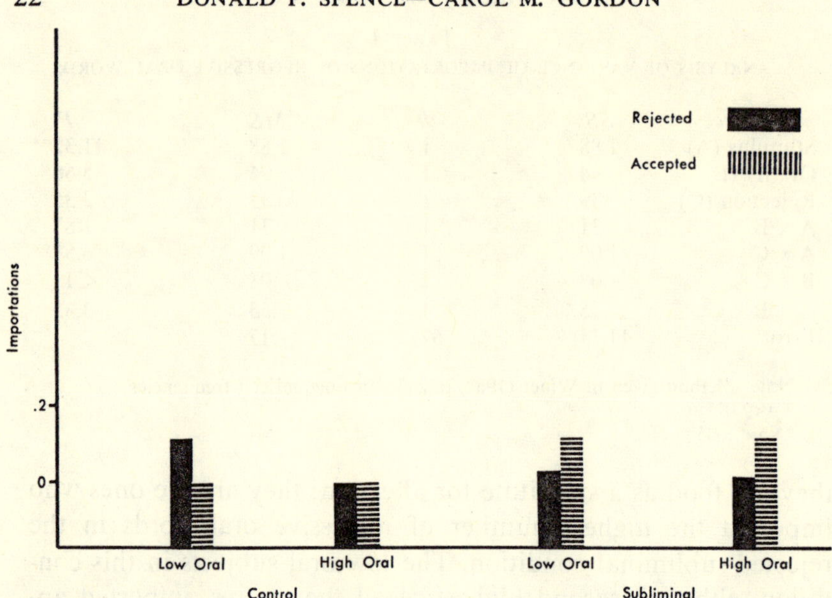

FIGURE 3. Importation of nonregressive oral words as a function of experimental rejection, subliminal stimulus, and level of orality.

cepted conditions. It also appears that rejection did not arouse a simple food fantasy: if it had, more food importations might have appeared in the rejected condition, and that was not the case.

The greater number of regressive oral importations suggests that the subliminal stimulus tends to activate derivatives which share some of the attributes of both fantasy and stimulus. They might be seen as a species of compromise formation, combining something of the initiating fantasy and something of the sensing instrument. "Mouth" and "bottle," for example, are better qualified for this role than "bread" and "water." It has also been suggested that the regressive oral importations might almost be characterized as symptoms. They have wish-fulfilling properties, for they are an expression of the fantasy, and from the subject's viewpoint they are also seemingly adaptive because they appear in the service of recall, the task required of him.

PATTERN OF RECALL

We now turn to the recall of the word list. The importations in recall showed the influence of both the oral fantasy and the subliminal stimulus, and we should expect to see a similar pattern in recall. The words related to the infantile feeding situation represent the best amalgam of the subliminal stimulus and the fantasy, and therefore they should emerge most strongly in recall when the fantasy was aroused and followed by a subliminal stimulus. We would expect to find these words most clearly recalled by the rejected-subliminal group.

For each subject we computed the difference between his recall of infantile milk associates (suck, mother, formula, etc.) and socialized milk associates (dairy, glass, butter, etc.). A positive difference (proportionately more infantile words recalled) would indicate that his recall of milk associates was biased toward the infantile end of the continuum.

The main findings are shown in Figure 4. For the high oral subjects, recall of infantile associates was greater in the rejected condition, particularly the rejected-subliminal condition, than in the accepted condition. Without the stimulus (high oral subjects in the rejected-control condition), infantile associates are not quite as much favored in recall, which is consistent with the

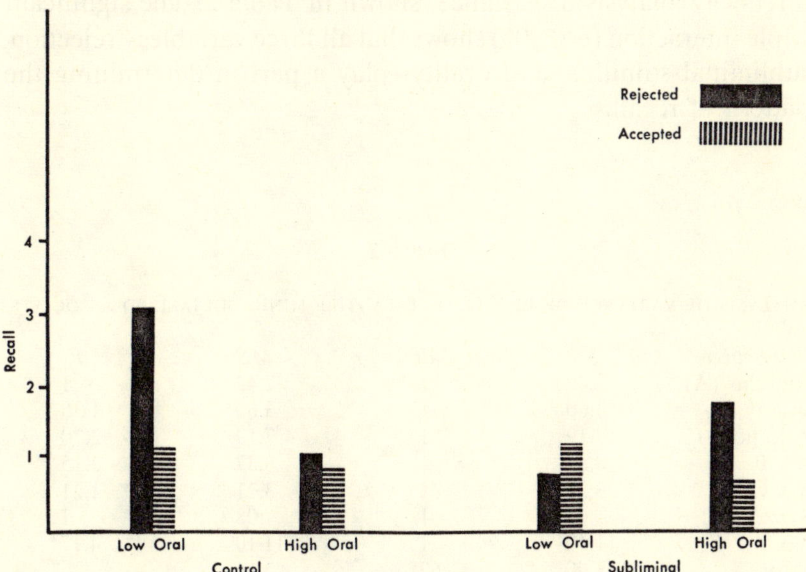

FIGURE 4. Recall of infantile minus socialized associates as a function of experimental rejection, subliminal stimulus, and level of orality.

hypothesis that without a mediating stimulus the fantasy undergoes more distortion as it is translated into derivatives. In this instance, the distortion is shown in the recall of more socialized derivatives.

In the low oral subjects, the pattern is strangely reversed. We can assume from their responses to the questionnaire that the low oral subjects are not aware of substituting food for affection; hence rejection would not be expected to arouse an oral fantasy, or at least not a highly regressed fantasy. The pattern of recall in low oral subjects in the rejected-subliminal condition seems to reflect such a socialized fantasy. What is surprising is that, in the control group, infantile associates are heavily favored in recall: by implication, the underlying fantasy is much more regressed. We hypothesized that without a mediating stimulus such a regressed fantasy would not emerge into awareness; the findings say otherwise. This is a question to be answered by further research; at the least, the findings in the control group do not conform to expectations. The findings in the subliminal condition, on the other hand, are more in line with the hypothesis.

The differences shown in Figure 4 were analyzed by a three-way analysis of variance, shown in Table 2. The significant triple interaction ($p < .05$) shows that all three variables—rejection, subliminal stimulus, and orality—play a part in determining the pattern of recall.

TABLE 2

ANALYSIS OF VARIANCE OF RECALL OF INFANTILE MINUS SOCIALIZED ASSOCIATES

Source	*SS*	*df*	*MS*	*F*
Stimulus (A)	2.42	1	2.42	<1
Orality (B)	3.60	1	3.60	1.35
Rejection (C)	7.19	1	7.19	2.70
A x B	8.37	1	8.37	3.15
A x C	3.21	1	3.21	1.21
B x C	.08	1	.08	1
A x B x C	11.10	1	11.10	4.17*
Error	178.00	67	2.66	

* $p < .05$

DISCUSSION

We started this study with two main propositions: (1) that a highly organized fantasy can be aroused outside of awareness; and (2) that a subliminal stimulus resembles a day residue in function, providing an entryway for material outside of awareness and allowing us to measure the aroused fantasy.

UNDERLYING FANTASY

What evidence do we have that an infantile fantasy was aroused by rejection? Two important reasons may be mentioned.

1. It seems consistent with what we know about the subjects from the questionnaire: the high oral subjects, by definition, use food as a response to rejection. They are also the ones who show the highest number of regressive oral importations, and it seems reasonable to assume that they respond to rejection with an unconscious oral fantasy.

2. The conceptual gap between rejection (loss of self-esteem) and the content of the importations (orally related words) cannot be explained simply in terms of the subliminal stimulus "milk." The stimulus alone might produce oral associates, but not necessarily a cluster related to early infantile experience. The biasing in this direction cannot simply be attributed to rejection, for what is there about a loss in self-esteem that would make for these associations? The gap seems most parsimoniously explained by the assumption that, in some subjects, rejection reproduced an earlier experience of deprivation which was answered at the time either by food or a conscious oral fantasy. This solution was eventually repressed and encapsulated in an unconscious fantasy which was triggered by the experimental rejection.

We might conclude that there is strong evidence that a fantasy was aroused but that its particular nature is undetermined. Our first proposition—that a highly organized fantasy can be aroused outside of awareness—must be declared not proven without further research. What about the second proposition—that a subliminal stimulus can provide an entryway for the fantasy?

FUNCTION OF THE SUBLIMINAL STIMULUS

It seems clear from the data on importations that a subliminal stimulus is necessary for the detection of an unconscious fantasy. All the high oral subjects in the rejected condition presumably had oral fantasies, but only in the rejected-subliminal condition did derivatives of these fantasies come into awareness. Not one high oral subject in the rejected-control condition imported even one regressive oral word. We presume that an oral fantasy was aroused in this condition but that, in the process of coming into awareness, it was idiosyncratically distorted to make it compatible with each subject's ego demands; the importations which did emerge, therefore, emerged silently, with no obvious oral characteristics to show that they were linked to the fantasy.

How does a subliminal stimulus facilitate the emergence of a fantasy? We can begin with the assumption developed above that an activated oral fantasy will influence the associates activated by an immediately following subliminal stimulus. These associates represent a restricted set of words, and the influence will produce an even further restriction, resulting in a set of words which has something in common with both the fantasy and the mediating stimulus. Only a relatively small number of words will fulfill these requirements, and perhaps that is why so many subjects imported the same words in the rejected-subliminal condition. The important point is that the subliminal stimulus, by means of its network of associates, provides an outlet for the unconscious fantasy. Because we assume all subjects have approximately the same network of associates, this outlet is widely shared and easily identified.

The associative network may have a protective function as well: by channeling all the activity of the fantasy through a set of ego-syntonic derivatives, it reduces the activation of the more anxiety-arousing derivatives which would lead, in turn, to increased censorship of the fantasy. Thus, the stimulus may provide a conflict-free path through which the fantasy can emerge.

Finally, the stimulus may facilitate emergence by reducing translation loss. Both the fantasy and the stimulus are outside of awareness and therefore share the same mode of organization. We know very little about the form in which a fantasy is represented outside of awareness, but it may well be that the same or a similar form is assumed by a verbal stimulus when it is registered outside of awareness. If so, the resulting congruence would give it a particular advantage as a measuring instrument.

The mediating effects of the subliminal stimulus were shown most clearly when we used the regressive oral importations as our response measure. Why were the importations so much more sensitive than the recall of infantile associates? The difference may stem from the fact that recall depends on attention and memory, two highly organized ego functions, whereas importations depend on lapses of attention and memory, and these lapses may reflect the pressure of unconscious material. We know from clinical work that derivatives of a fantasy are more likely to emerge when the patient is in a partially relaxed, introspective, and uncritical state. We challenge this state when we ask for recall of all possible words, and we support it when we encourage guessing. It is not surprising, therefore, that the subject's guesses provided better evidence of the underlying fantasy than did his disciplined recall, which argues for a future procedure in which only a fragmented word list is presented whose main function is to elicit importations.

CONCLUSION

Unconscious fantasies are often inferred from behavior in the treatment situation, but they rarely appear in a form that can be measured or studied for long periods. Taking advantage of the fact that a subliminal stimulus is, by definition, outside of awareness, it was hypothesized that it would provide a point of entry for an unconscious fantasy, much as the day residue is believed to enable the unconscious wish to emerge in the dream. With such a mediating subliminal stimulus, we would expect the unconscious fantasy to appear in consciousness in a relatively undistorted form. Inferences about the underlying fantasy based on these derivatives would, accordingly, be less subject to error.

To test this proposition, we hypothesized that severe rejection would arouse a compensating unconscious fantasy of being fed. Such a fantasy would be particularly likely to appear among subjects who showed, on a questionnaire, that they use food in response to rejection. High- and low-scoring subjects on this questionnaire were divided into four groups. Two of these groups were made to feel rejected and two made to feel accepted. One rejected group was exposed to a subliminal oral stimulus, the word "milk," immediately after being rejected, and the other was exposed to a blank slide. Correspondingly, one accepted group was shown the subliminal stimulus, and the other the blank slide. All subjects were then asked to learn a list of words, some related to the infantile nursing situation and some related to a more socialized eating situation.

It was expected that rejection would arouse an oral fantasy in all subjects, but that it would appear most clearly in the rejected-subliminal subgroup where the subliminal stimulus could facilitate the entry of the fantasy into awareness. Within this subgroup, high-scoring subjects on the oral questionnaire were expected to show a stronger effect than low-scoring subjects. The hypothesis was most strongly confirmed in the analysis of importations—words which were not on the word list but were erroneously recalled. Four findings are worthy of note: (1) Regressive oral importations (i.e., milk, bottle, mouth, nipple, smell, and taste) were much more frequent in the rejected-subliminal condition than in any other condition. (2) Within the rejected-subliminal group, high oral subjects imported many more regressive words than did low oral subjects. (3) In the absence of rejection, the subliminal stimulus did not appreciably increase the number of regressive importations. (4) Without a subliminal stimulus, rejection alone did not appreciably increase the number of regressive importations. Thus the effects of rejection—namely, the derivatives of an unconscious oral fantasy—did not clearly emerge in awareness unless a subliminal stimulus had also been presented.

These and other findings have been discussed with reference to two main questions: (1) Can a highly organized fantasy be aroused outside of awareness? (2) Can a subliminal stimulus function as a day residue and provide an entry point for material outside of awareness?

2

FORGETTING AND REMEMBERING (MOMENTARY FORGETTING) DURING PSYCHOTHERAPY: A NEW SAMPLE

LESTER LUBORSKY

No matter how good one's memory, lapses into states of forgetfulness occur in which various forms of forgetting may appear. In one very fleeting form, the thought which had just been in awareness drops out but often is quickly recovered. This form I call, therefore, *momentary* forgetting. It has a uniform structure:

1. A report of awareness of having forgotten a thought; e.g., "Oh, I just had a thought and I don't know what it was; it slipped out of my mind."

2. A brief pause for an effort at recovery of the thought.

3. (a) A report of recovery of the thought; e.g., "Ah! Here it is . . ." Or: (b) "It's gone, and I can't bring it back."

Once a patient of mine in psychotherapy momentarily forgot a thought at a serendipitous moment. A flash of insight into the context of the patient's forgetting came to me. Then I got a vision of the promise of such experiences for research in memory and in psychotherapy. Here was a recurrent experience in which

The work reported in this chapter was supported in part by United States Public Health Service Grant No. MH-15442 and Scientist Award No. K05-MH-40110. The author wishes to acknowledge the help of Philip G. Mechanick, Shirly Heinemann, Merton Gill, Justin Simon, Donald Spence, Ulrich Neisser, Johannes Ipsen, Martin Orne, Jacob Cohen, Freda M. Greene, Donald Phoenix, Marcia Polsky, Roberta B. Harvey, Theresa Lynch, Herbert Weissman, Geraldine Fink, Robert Holt, and James Mintz.

An earlier version of this chapter was presented at the American Psychological Association Symposium of September, 1966; the present slightly revised version was presented at the meeting of the Rapaport Study Group at the Austen Riggs Center, Stockbridge, Massachusetts, in June, 1968.

a thought that is intended to be spoken is first forgotten and then often remembered. I realized that a psychotherapist listening over many years might profitably collect such instances with no special equipment except *patience* and *patients.*

Other forms of forgetting appear in the ebb and flow of thoughts in a free-association session or in any psychotherapy session, but *momentary* forgetting was chosen because of (1) its regularity of form; (2) its nearly universal occurrence; and (3) the completeness and rapidity of the forgetting-remembering sequence–the loss of a thought is quickly followed by its retrieval.

Probably because of its brevity and seemingly inconsequential nature, the momentary forgetting phenomenon has never received any research attention. A search of the clinical, theoretical, and experimental literature turned up nothing on this type of forgetting. Freud's *The Psychopathology of Everyday Life* (1901), with its many examples of forgetting, includes none on *momentary* forgetting.

PILOT STUDY

I began a private pilot study (Luborsky, 1964, 1967). In my process notes of each session I included all forms of memory disturbance, especially occurrences of momentary forgetting, transcribed verbatim. The first series of observations involved 19 patients, 2,085 sessions, and a total of 69 instances of forgetting, two thirds of them being ones in which the thought was recovered approximately as it had been originally thought, according to the patients' willingness and ability to report. Of the 19 patients, only four had no momentary forgetting. The frequency of momentary forgetting instances was one in 30 sessions. Two patients had the highest frequency: one in 10 sessions. Momentary forgetting lasted from one or two seconds to about 70 seconds from the onset of the forgetting to the beginning of recall, or to the giving up of trying to recall.

I first tried to classify the recurrent theme for each of the 15 patients who had shown any momentary forgetting into one of four types: *sexual, anger, control and competence,* or *lack of control and competence.* Classification was quite easy because the themes seemed consistent across occasions within a patient. Each of the first three themes fitted a few patients; the last theme fitted the majority—that is, within each patient *lack of control and competence* was the most frequently recurrent theme of momentary forgetting.

The next analysis was based upon ratings of the two- or 3-sentence context adjacent to the momentary forgetting compared with ratings of matched control contexts. Thirty-seven segments of the process notes containing momentary forgetting were matched with 37 control segments. The ratings were based upon 12 (six content and six formal) categories (Luborsky, 1967). The content categories were: sex, anger, control and competence, lack of control and competence, guilt, and oedipal conflict. The formal categories were: level of abstraction, observation of self, important relationships, new attitude, elated mood, and difficulty with attention. The qualities of contexts which were most discriminating in order of the size of their *t* were: *(1) new attitude or behavior; (2) difficulty with attention; (3) guilt; (4) lack of control and competence; (5) oedipal conflict.*

The same ratings were then applied only to the recovered versus control words, rather than to the adjacent larger context of sentences described in the preceding paragraph. The discriminating categories for the recovered words alone were approximately the same as those for the larger context, with the addition of *high level of abstraction, observation about oneself, references to an important relationship,* and *an elated mood.* Apparently, therefore, the thoughts that are recovered are not new ones suddenly emerging, but only slight variations of the surrounding thought context, such as a specification or an epitome of the thought.

CROSS-VALIDATION STUDY

It took the unhurried, unmanipulative temperament of a naturalist to make the original pilot collection and to see whether the specimens had features in common; about three years were consumed. As much as one would want to manufacture a reliable supply of these instances of forgetting, it seemed too early for the talents of a "biochemist" or a "psychopharmacologist" who would try to precipitate such behavior analogues in the laboratory. The method at that time was phenomenological, non-

"brass-instrument," and based only on my own patients. But my nagging conscience and aspirations told me that I had better move to methods which are "now" and do a cross-validation study, because, if I did not, what I had discovered might be permanently forgotten.

My first observations of momentary forgetting phenomena were recorded by writing, either as the patient spoke or immediately after the session ended. In recognition of the fleeting nature of the behavior and the fallibility of the therapist-listener as a recording instrument, a tape recorder was added to the equipment armamentarium. The new collection now includes material from 10 patients, each of whom gave two or more specimens of momentary forgetting, preserved on tape, ready for re-examination exactly as they occurred. Five of the 10 were treated by other therapists, and five by the author. Inclusion of other therapists' patients should prevent the results from being the unique product of one therapist. In addition, for one patient we have a sample of 13 passable instances of momentary forgetting over a period of 300 sessions. In summary, we can now carry out a precise group analysis across the 10 patients, as well as one intensive within-patient analysis.

My present and long-term aims have been: (1) to examine a type of naturally occurring forgetting within the context of psychotherapy; (2) to develop and demonstrate appropriate quantitative methods for showing a high degree of lawfulness in an easily defined clinical phenomenon; (3) to apply the method to test the findings of a pilot clinical study of momentary forgetting (Luborsky, 1964, 1967); (4) to determine whether the concept of repression appears to be useful in explaining the data of momentary forgetting; (5) to apply the methods to recurrent somatic symptoms appearing during psychotherapy.

METHODS OF DATA ANALYSIS

Every momentary forgetting session was matched with a control session, arbitrarily defined as one occurring either five sessions earlier or five sessions later, with as many control sessions in the earlier as in the later position. In terms of the number of psychotherapy sessions that must be taped, collecting a sufficient number of momentary forgettings is a sizable job. However, the participating therapists were all tape-recording their psychotherapy sessions for other purposes as well—for psychotherapy research or for teaching purposes.

The huge mountain of data can be reduced to a more easily scaled foothill by focusing on the momentary forgetting sessions and the control sessions, and then on only a portion of each session. The first step in the data analysis is marking the site of the initiation of the momentary forgetting, arbitrarily located at the beginning of the pause before the patient says, "I forgot what I was going to say." The surrounding 1,000 [1] words of the patient are counted: 500 words before the momentary forgetting and 500 words after it. These units are each divided into 50-word segments, so that there are 10 50-word segments before the forgetting and 10 segments after it. They occupy about six minutes before the forgetting and six minutes after it. The 1,000 words are then analyzed by a variety of content-analysis methods, and the scores for the 50-word segments are plotted on graphs.

Within each control session a "control point" must be designated, as far into the control tape (minutes and seconds) as the matched momentary forgetting is situated. After the control point in the control session is established, 10 50-word segments are counted off before and after it. These methods of selecting control sessions and control points are objective ones—to prevent experimenter bias in choosing control samples, and to control for position in the session of the selected word sample.

All momentary forgetting sessions and control sessions are transcribed. Portions around the forgetting point or the control point are carefully listened to by another person, independently, and are further corrected so that the transcript accurately reflects the patient's actual expressions—with all the "ohs" and "ahs," slips, pauses, mispronunciations, and emphases.

METHODS OF QUALITY CONTROL IN THE SELECTION OF MOMENTARY FORGETTING INSTANCES

One penalty for relying on a naturalistic method for picking up specimens where one finds them is their natural variability. A

[1] For some analyses this number is extended to 1,100 or reduced to 600 words.

good way to cope with this is to grade each example for its degree of fit to a defined ideal form.

Fortunately, the behavior shows much stereotypy, which makes it easier to find an ideal form. The exact point of onset of the momentary forgetting is usually well marked. The patient, who has been speaking, stops, pauses, and explains (as in Session 20 of Patient X; see Appendix), "I lost the other point that I was about to make." The point of onset is taken as the beginning of the pause before the explanation. To be more exact, the point of onset is taken as the time after the last word which is equal to the usual pause the patient makes between words. The statement, "I lost the other point that I was going to make," or "I forgot what I was going to say," is to try to explain what is happening during the pause, and why the person cannot go on with the sentence he started or the thought he intended to express.

The crucial aspect of adequacy, which must be present to some degree before any instance of momentary forgetting can be accepted, is that the thought must have been present before it vanished. The more fully it is articulated before the loss, the better. Other aspects which seemed relevant, but were not considered crucial in estimating adequacy, were:

1. The suddenness of the loss of the thought. It usually can be taken as further evidence that the patient has been faithfully reporting his thoughts immediately before the forgetting.

2. The patient's spontaneous effort to recover the lost thought. The amount of effort seems to indicate the presence of a true disruption of the patient's associations. The patient finds it difficult to go on unless an effort is made to recover the thought and continue from where he left off.

3. The absence of external distraction. Instances of obvious external distraction are rare. When one occurs, the therapist usually seems to be responsible for it, by his prodding or interruption.

Retrieval of the lost thought is not considered necessary for defining momentary forgetting because in the pilot study I was not able to find any differences between contexts with recovery and contexts without recovery.

There must be an *explicit* indication of the crucial quality: that the thought was present before it vanished. Nonexplicit momentary forgettings may sometimes occur, and there may be some risk in discarding such presumed instances; but there would be more risk if they were included.

RESULTS OF THE STUDY OF THE NEW SAMPLE OF 10 PATIENTS

So far, three variables suggested by the pilot work have been explored: (1) *attention difficulties (cognitive disturbances);* (2) *anxiety;* (3) *relationship with the therapist.* This choice of variables was determined by the promise of each, as well as by our ability to translate some aspects of it into a reliable measure. A section of the results is devoted to each of these variables.

1. Do cognitive disturbances build up before the appearance of momentary forgetting?

On the basis of the pilot study, two main conditions were thought to be essential for momentary forgetting: (1) contact of a thought with a derivative of a drive-organized memory system; (2) the presence of a "distracted state" in the few minutes before and after the forgetting, and possibly in the entire session. Together, these conditions should produce attention difficulties. In addition, and because momentary forgetting is, in itself, one form of memory function disturbance, it seemed reasonable to expect a variety of related types of cognitive disturbance to occur before the forgetting. Three broad classes of disturbances were observed: forgetting and near forgetting; indications of uncertainty about one's thoughts; unclarity and confusion about expressing them. A scoring manual was created which lists 25 subtypes of disturbance, with examples of each. The score is the sum of the number of instances of the 25 categories of disturbance. The scoring manual has been labeled "A Cognitive Disturbance Measure" (Luborsky, 1966), but the label may have to be altered because the "uncertainty" categories have been the most frequently scored. Preliminary tests indicate that reliability is moderately high, which is no surprise, since the discretion left to the judge is small.

The scored segment of patient's speech consisted of 500 words before and after the momentary forgetting for each of the 26 forgetting and control examples. The results clearly show the

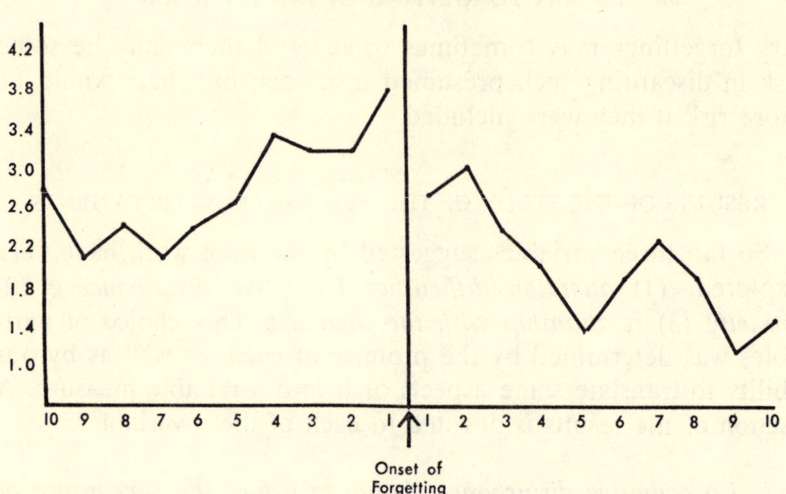

FIGURE 1. Fifty-word units of patients' speech: *cognitive disturbance* scores before and after momentary forgetting (means for 10 patients; momentary forgetting instances, averaged by patient, scored by independent judge).

expectations to have been correct: there is an upward trend in the cognitive disturbance scores for the 10 successive 50-word units of the 500-word segment (Figure 1). After the forgetting, the curve declines. One test of the upward trend would be to compare the amount of cognitive disturbance in the 150 words *just before* the forgetting with the 150 words *at the start of the 500-word unit.* A Wilcoxon Signed Rank Test of the differences is significant (at between .025 and .01 levels; one-tailed test). (Before computation, each subject's scores had been averaged so that all subjects had the same chance of contributing to the results.)

Another Wilcoxon Test [2]—this time of the entire inverted V-shaped curve—was highly significant (.005 level, one-tailed test): differences between amount of cognitive disturbance *adjacent* to the forgetting (in the 150 words immediately before and 150 words immediately after the forgetting) versus *distal* to the forgetting (in the sum of the two 150-word units farthest from

[2] These Wilcoxon Tests on 150 words will be supplemented by more complete statistical tests of the trends. The Wilcoxon may be wasteful—it may capitalize on flukes in the curve, and does not use all the data. Among other analyses, we will try a correlation of the cognitive disturbance score for each 50-word unit with the temporal position number of that unit.

the forgetting). The control sessions showed none of these significant differences.[3]

In sum, to utter 150 words during psychotherapy takes most patients about two minutes. The highest rate of cognitive disturbance is in the two minutes before and the two minutes after the momentary forgetting–but especially before.

This is a good moment to mention that momentary forgetting rarely occurs in the first 20 minutes of a session. The peak frequency of onset is approximately 20 minutes after the session has started. One implication of this fact may be that it takes time to get involved enough with the therapist to begin to speak about a threatening content from which one can be (or needs to be) distracted by forgetting.

2. Is the supposed build-up of anxiety before forgetting reflected in increased speech disturbance?

Anxiety, or at least "signal anxiety," is supposed to act in the precipitation of forgetting, according to Freud's theory of symptom formation (1926). The "at least" is intended to convey that Freud's theory states that there need only be minute anxiety–just sufficient to signal the imminence of a dangerous thought. Our assessment devices, therefore, may not catch much anxiety, and negative results would say little to refute the theory.

One may find, however, that a function as sensitive as speech will be disrupted by even small quantities of anxiety. Mahl (1956) has shown that his "non-ah" measure of speech disturbance tends to vary with fluctuations of anxiety in interviews. Mahl's measure is the sum of instances of seven types of speech disruption: sentence correction, incomplete sentence, word repetition, stuttering, intruding incoherent sounds, slips of the tongue, and omissions of words or parts of words. Would scores on his measure jump up just before and after the forgetting? Would the shape of the curve be similar to that for cognitive disturbances?

[3] The rate of cognitive disturbances for the *entire prior-500-word* segment is also significantly higher than the rate in the entire post-500 words. My speculations about this are not convincing. Perhaps the imminence of the threatening content is responsible not only for the momentary forgetting but also for a subsequent period of relative reintegration and control–or at least a decline of cognitive disturbance.

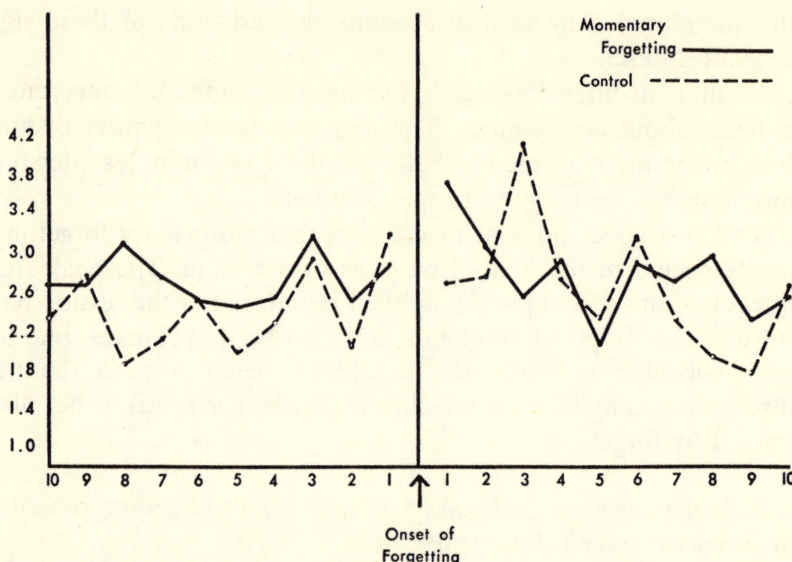

FIGURE 2. Fifty-word units of patients' speech: *speech disturbance* scores before and after momentary forgetting (means for 10 patients; 26 momentary forgetting instances, averaged by patient, scored by independent judge).

The results turned out to be negative—the curve for speech disturbance in each 50-word unit (independently scored by another judge) is essentially flat before the forgetting and almost the same after the forgetting (Figure 2). For the control contexts, the findings were nonsignificant before the forgetting, but just after the control onset point there was an inexplicable significant drop in speech disturbance (by Wilcoxon Test).

What seemed like a fairly good hunch about the appearance of speech disturbances, therefore, did not work out.

3. How is relationship with the therapist involved in the patient's momentary forgetting experience?

As indicated by the earlier study, a necessary condition for momentary forgetting is the contact of a train of thought with a derivative of a repressed memory system. The contact sets off a danger signal to the patient about knowing and expressing the thought *in the presence of the therapist. In the presence of the therapist* is emphasized because it is a crucial ingredient. No matter whether the theme is sexual, or aggressive, or describes lack of control (the most consistent intraindividual themes in the previous study), an important element seems to be the patient's compunction about saying or thinking something in the presence of the therapist. Even when the patient does not explicitly mention the therapist, the transference meanings of the intended-to-be-expressed thought seem crucial in determining the forgetting.

In the pilot sample we had noted the frequency of references to important relationships; in the tape-recorded sample we began to be impressed by the frequency of explicit reference to the relationship with the therapist. For Patient X in Session 20 (see Appendix), the momentary forgetting came just after she had the thought that the therapist was judging her as not being amenable to treatment. In Session 36 the patient is again directly referring to the therapist. In Session 53 the patient makes clear her reference to the therapist, stating that what she had been saying just before the forgetting "was the same kind of feeling I'd had when I couldn't understand why *you* did something." The momentary forgetting in Sessions 66 and 83 also involves direct references to the therapist. Only Session 91 does not.

How frequently does one find, in the 26 examples, explicit reference to feelings about the therapist? Is explicit reference to the therapist as frequent in the control contexts?

To simplify the first minimal analysis, only the 150 words before and the 150 words after the onset of forgetting were culled, and only for explicit references involving feelings toward the therapist. Sixteen of the 26 momentary forgetting examples include explicit reference to the therapist; only three of the 14 control examples contain explicit reference to the therapist ($X^2 = 5.94$, significant between .02 and .01 levels).

An independent judge then rated the amount of explicit reference to the therapist in each of six 50-word units before the onset of the forgetting. To rate blindly required that the judge not see the transcript after the point of onset of forgetting and not know which transcripts were of forgetting sessions and which were controls. Figure 3 shows that the amount of explicit reference to the therapist is greater in the forgetting sessions than it is in the controls, starting approximately 150 words before the onset of the forgetting. Only the 50-word unit closest to the forget-

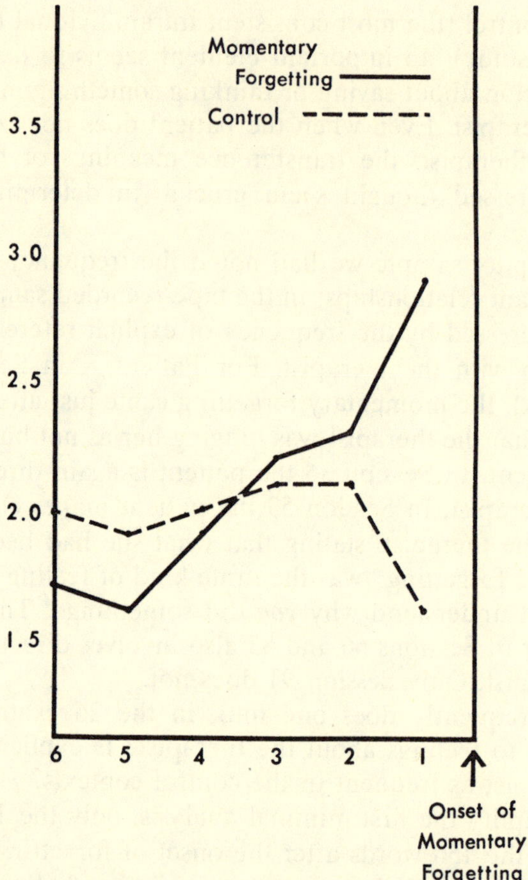

FIGURE 3. Fifty-word units of patients' speech: *explicit reference to the therapist* scores before momentary forgetting (means for 10 patients; 26 momentary forgetting instances and 26 controls, scored by independent judge).

ting shows a significantly larger number of explicit references to the therapist in the forgetting sessions than in the controls ($p < .05$).

An exploration of the *nature* of the reference to the therapist was begun. A category was created called *involvement with the therapist*, and each of the 50-word segments was rated on it by an independent judge.[4] Figure 4 shows that the curve is similar; that is, at approximately 150 words before the onset of forget-

[4] The same rater scored several other variables: *guilt, separation* concern, *anger to therapist*, and *rejection*. Results were nonsignificant.

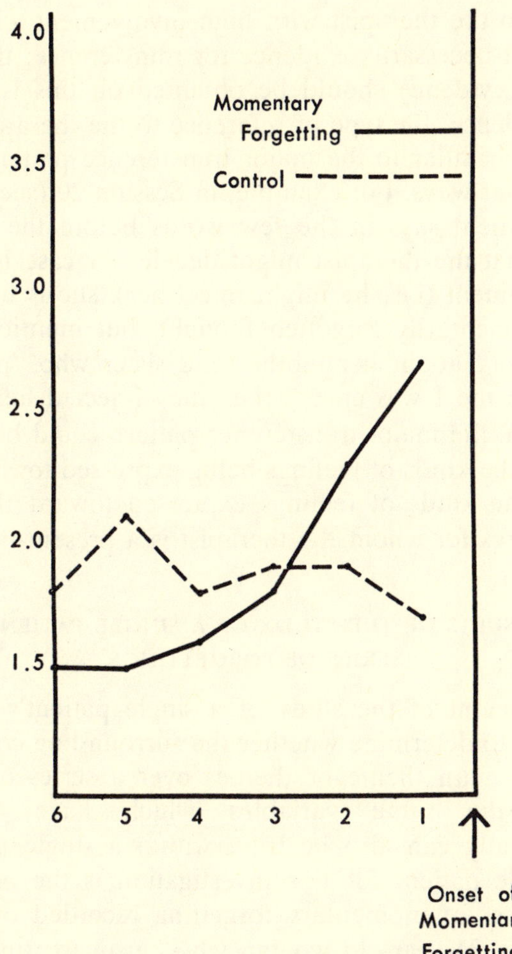

FIGURE 4. Fifty-word units of patients' speech: *involvement with therapist* scores before momentary forgetting (means for 10 patients; 26 momentary forgetting instances and 26 controls, scored by independent judge).

ting, involvement with the therapist is significantly higher in the forgetting sessions than in the controls ($p < .05$). (In subsequent work, more raters will be added and a further study will be made of other types of reference to the therapist.)

It might have been expected that heightened involvement in the transference would be associated with momentary forgetting. What was surprising was the frequency with which the reference to the therapist was explicit around that time. These explicit references to the therapist with high involvement with the therapist are not necessarily evidence for transference: they may be, but further evidence should be obtained on this issue. As one form of evidence, the type of reference to the therapist might be shown to be similar to the major transference patterns as established in other ways. For example, in Session 20 (see Appendix), after the patient says in the few words before the momentary forgetting that the therapist might decide her case is not amenable to treatment (i.e., he might reject her), she is unable to recall the momentarily forgotten thought, but mentions an associated memory about her mother and sister who "made fun of me and told me I was crazy" (i.e., they rejected her). For each patient, then, the major transference pattern could be listed both in terms of the kinds of feelings being expressed toward the therapist and the kinds of feelings expressed toward the probable archaic figures for whom the therapist is a present-day stand-in.

RESULTS OF THE STUDY OF A SINGLE PATIENT'S SERIES OF FORGETTINGS

The main aim of the study of a single patient's momentary forgetting is to determine whether the surrounding contexts show a consistent main theme or themes over a series of occasions. Some of the same variables which have been tried cross-sectionally can also be tried within a single patient. The most suitable patient for this investigation is the one with the most instances of momentary forgetting recorded on tape. The patient was a 31-year-old woman who began treatment because of her concern about a series of attachments to men, all of whom were much younger than she, all of whom were unsuitable, by all of whom she felt unfairly treated, and with all of whom she eventually terminated her relationship.

By reading and rereading the instances and contexts, I became attuned to the theme of her struggles. It is easy to discern the theme, even in the 25 or 30 words before each of the first six momentary forgettings[5] (see Appendix). The thoughts preceding

[5] Only the first six examples from a sample of 13 from this patient are presented here; other findings are abbreviated, in view of a larger report on this patient (Luborsky and Mintz, in press).

all the forgettings are about her relationship with a man; in five of the six, the man is explicitly the therapist. In all of them the man is rejecting her or is considerately managing to avoid rejecting her. The man is not liking her or liking her. In essence, the momentary forgetting is a moment of truth in which is revealed what a man feels for her, or what she feels for a man. In Session 20, the forgetting follows her thought that the therapist is going to say that she is not amenable to treatment. In Session 36, the loss of the thought follows a slip in which the patient said, "I present myself to you in such a way that I can't like you." (She meant to say "that you can't like me"; the slip reveals her hostility toward the therapist.) In Session 53, the lost thought follows the patient's raising the possibility that the boy she has been dating hates his father, and "I don't *really* think it applies to me." In Session 66, the preceding thought was that *now* when the therapist says the time is up, she realizes he does not mean to reject her. In Session 83, the patient is considering how she would feel if the therapist forgot her session. In Session 91, there is another near slip—the patient says, "I seem very nicely to have picked on men who get in my way." She meant to say "who don't treat me well"; the "get in my way" is evidence of the intrusion of the patient's hostility toward men.

Figure 5 presents the average ratings by two independent judges on a 5-point scale which ranged from *no rejection* to *very much rejection. Rejection* is defined as a negative response to the patient given by another person. The negative response takes the form of dislike or lack of interest, withholding of something, evaluating the patient as inadequate, or revealing the intention to break off with the patient. The denial of rejection is scored on the same scale; that is, a rejection score is also given when the patient stresses that the rejector "was *not* rejecting me." The scale is therefore one of preoccupation with the theme of rejection, whether it is considered to be present or whether its absence is stressed. (This rejection theme appears to be a specific form of the larger theme described as the most common one in the pilot study; that is, *lack of control or competence.*) The outstanding finding shown in Figure 5 is that the level of rejection is consistently higher in the momentary forgetting segments than in

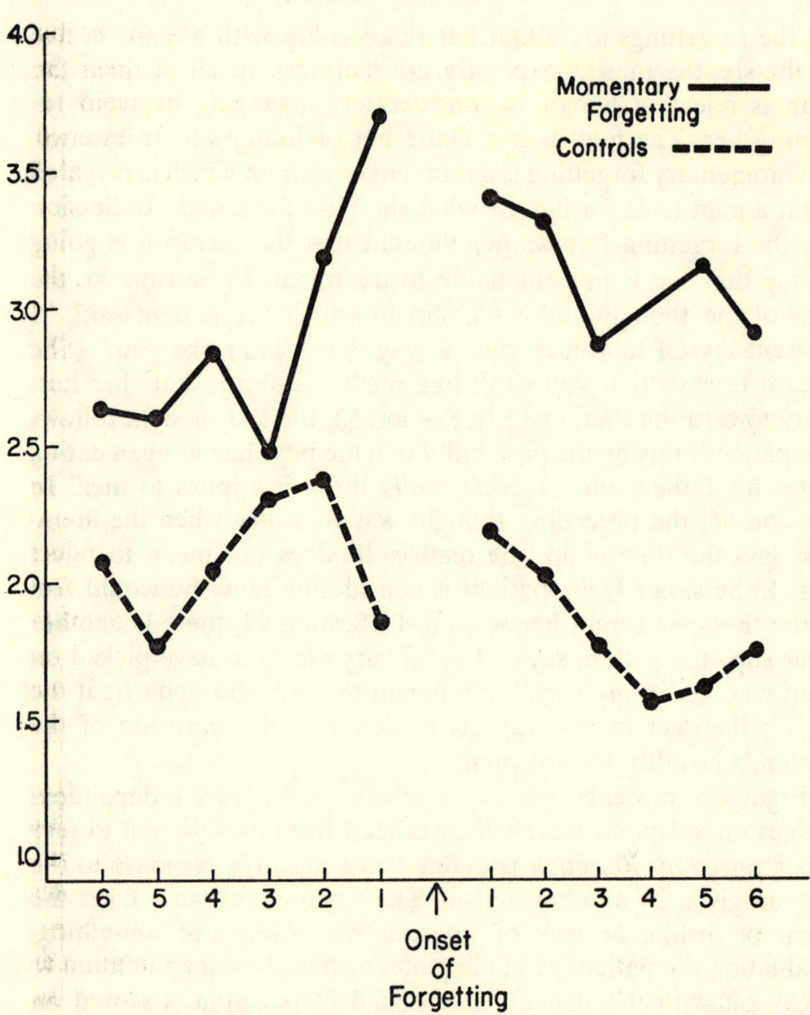

FIGURE 5. Fifty-word units of one patient's speech: *rejection* scores before and after momentary forgetting (mean of 13 momentary forgetting instances and 13 controls, scored by two independent judges).

the control segments for the total of 600 words—the 300 words before and the 300 words after the forgetting.

If the concept of repression were to apply to the momentary forgetting data, one expectation would be that the momentary forgetting contexts would repeatedly contain one main theme. There is convincing evidence for a single main rejection theme.

A second expectation would be that the theme would be prominent in independent assessments of drive-organized memory systems; for example, those based on early memories, dreams, and TAT stories. We have not yet made independent assessments of drive-organized memory systems for Patient X; however, even at this point one outstanding conclusion seems warranted: the recurrent theme of rejection, especially rejection by a man, appears to be pervasive and may be considered to be the core of her conflicts. We might go so far as to say, therefore, that for Patient X the repeated theme is not only a central one, but appears to be based on a drive-organized memory system which is at the heart of the therapeutic problem even as identified by the patient in listing her own symptoms during the first few sessions of treatment. In Session 1 the patient says, "The thing that originally made me seek therapy was that I was in an unusually emotional state, with crying and depression . . . and an encounter with a young man touched or culminated the whole thing." In Session 2 the patient says, again describing the circumstances that led her to apply for treatment, "I wrote a prospectus for the dissertation . . . I got very tense. I just felt on the brink of falling apart at certain moments and then I had the feeling one morning after I finished typing this prospectus. I'd been up all night. I was afraid I was gonna have an hallucination that I was gonna see a man that didn't really exist." In the same session the patient adds, "I've become quite withdrawn, afraid of getting involved with people. I have these bizarre thoughts. The other day I ran into someone in the street. We talked for a few minutes. He said, 'We'll see each other again.' But the thought crossed my mind that I will hurt him again. So, naturally, I'm not very eager to see him again." In Session 4 the patient mentions that her first contact with a therapist (just before the analysis) was one in which the therapist "pointed out I always set up the relationship with men, or I always choose one which I could feel terrible anger against, and that I would be forbearing, and accept the conditions as laid down by them, meekly on the surface, but meanwhile would be feeling very resentful and ill-treated." According to the supervisor of the analysis, around the time of the 300th session (the last information we have), the central therapeutic problem remains to deal with the patient's disbelief in the good intentions of the analyst toward her. This was described by the supervisor as the issue that would have to be resolved before the treatment could be successful.

To show more convincingly that there is only one main theme would require examination of the contexts from many different perspectives. This is being done; there is good evidence so far that *rejection* is the most prominently consistent theme. Although a high degree of *involvement with the therapist* is also discriminat-

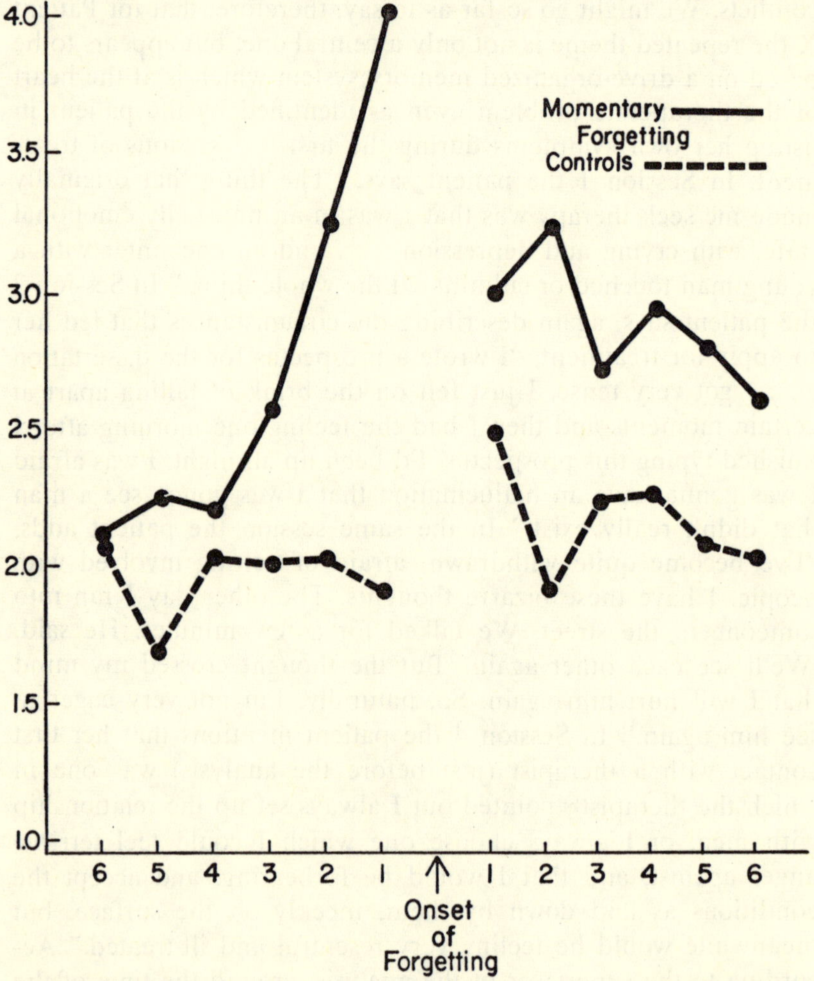

FIGURE 6. Fifty-word units of one patient's speech: *involvement with therapist* scores before and after momentary forgetting (mean of 13 momentary forgetting instances and 13 controls, scored by two independent judges).

ing (Figure 6), the involvement is obviously concerned with *rejection* by the therapist. *Helplessness* and *hostility* also turn out to be involved (Luborsky and Mintz, in press).

SUMMARY AND DISCUSSION

In this study I have tried to contribute to the research on memory disturbance and to psychoanalytic research methods at three levels:

1. By showing lawfulness in a well-defined, naturally occurring memory phenomenon, momentary forgetting, which has not previously been studied.
2. By presenting a set of tools for the analysis of such symptomatic behaviors in interview settings, especially the systematic comparison of forgetting with control contexts and the creation of reliable measures, such as that for cognitive disturbance. Studies of physical as well as psychological symptoms which appear in interviews have been poorly controlled; our methods have special suitability for such research (Luborsky and Auerbach, 1969; Luborsky, 1970).
3. By demonstrating a way of testing a psychoanalytic concept in a nonlaboratory context, where information relevant to the theory might conceivably be discerned.

If we are able to show that a common memory disturbance can be examined in a controlled way in the context of a patient's thoughts, we may help to diversify and objectify the research style in psychoanalysis. Psychoanalysis needs this widening of the channels to the rest of psychology. When forgetting appears during psychoanalysis or psychotherapy, the therapist is there as an observer and the tape recorder is a witness to the verbal interaction of the patient and the therapist. Because of the nature of the psychotherapeutic relationship, there is a good chance that the patient's thoughts surrounding the forgetting will be explicit. The method for studying momentary forgetting represents an attempt to grapple with the complexity of a clinical phenomenon by finding ways of simply and systematically reducing the data. The method represents an alternative to seeking to create analogues of repression in the laboratory in the manner of the experiments reviewed by Madison (1956), Sears (1943, 1944), and others.

Their reviews showed the difficulty and generally disappointing results of the laboratory-analogues approach. "It's not really a test of the theory" is the response of those who think in psychoanalytic terms (and who bother to investigate the experimental literature on the subject). Those who are not thinking psychoanalytically retain their belief that the concept of repression is not useful.

DIFFICULTIES IN APPLYING THE CONCEPT OF REPRESSION TO MOMENTARY FORGETTING

My aims of describing momentary forgetting as a phenomenon and of developing methods for its elucidation seem easier to accomplish than the aim of testing the fit of the concept of repression to these data. To explain the momentary forgetting phenomenon, there are two main competing hypotheses: (1) repression; (2) external distraction.

By *external distraction* is meant an overload or diversion of attention caused by the therapist, by a noise, etc. If distraction were the single determinant, one would not expect to find any theoretically predictable regularity in the points at which momentary forgetting occurs; e.g., the context would not be related to drive-organized memory systems.

I tried to see the extent to which inferences from the theory of repression fit the observations about momentary forgetting. If the concept of repression (or any defensive process) is applicable to momentary forgetting, the following general interpretive framework should be demonstrable: *When forgetting appears, the stream of the patient's associations has just made contact with a specific thought which then threatens to intrude into unwelcoming awareness. The specific threatening thought would be part of what Rapaport (1951a) has called "a drive-organized memory system."* This interpretive framework needs to be translated into specific expectations of what should appear in the momentary forgetting data:

1. If momentary forgetting is associated with one of the patient's major repressed memory systems (rather than appearing on a random distraction basis), one main theme should recurrently appear in the surrounding context.

2. If one theme recurrently appears in a series of a patient's momentary forgettings, that theme should be prominent in independent assessments of drive-organized memory systems (based on early memories, dreams, and TAT stories).

3. If repressed memory systems or complexes have been highly activated just before momentary forgetting, one might expect to find more immediately experienced transference manifestations; that is, the main theme in the forgetting context will be expressed in the relationship with the therapist. It is difficult to estimate transference quantitatively, but a rating scheme applied by independent examiners might be able to identify the type and the immediacy of the transference (Luborsky, Graff, Pulver, and Curtis, in press). One might also try objectively measurable, though oversimplified, estimates of transference activity; e.g., frequency of explicit references to the therapist.

4. If for some time before the momentary forgetting, threatening thoughts are about to intrude into awareness, one might find evidence of cognitive strain and disturbance during that time. If a repressive mechanism applies to momentary forgetting, it seems unlikely that the repressive forces instigating the forgetting could operate so discretely as to leave no generalized stigmata. The pilot study, in fact, revealed a variety of disruptions such as "attention disturbances." I was led to the conclusion that a necessary precondition for momentary forgetting was a *distracted state.* Klein (1967, especially p. 112, under "Motivational Attributes of Repressed Trains of Thought") stresses this view. He points out that repression does not necessarily implicate memory. It may involve many other qualities, such as the state of consciousness, obsessiveness, and a sense of the uncanny. The patient may have a harder time knowing what he is thinking. He may forget more, or show signs that he is on the verge of forgetting. He may be more uncertain about his thoughts, and may have a harder time expressing his thoughts clearly. A 25-item cognitive disturbance manual has therefore been constructed, which includes instances of forgetting and near forgetting, uncertainty, and unclarity (Luborsky, 1966).

5. If threatening thoughts are about to intrude into awareness, one may expect to find anxiety building up before the momentary forgetting. However, the general theory does not directly

lead to only one expectation; before measurable anxiety develops, forgetting or some defense may intervene. The anxiety level may be minimal, with only "signal anxiety" to warn that a threatening thought is emerging. It is not reasonable to suppose that all patients will deal with their threatening thoughts in the same way. Some may show heightened anxiety, while others may quickly contain their anxiety by a defensive maneuver such as isolation. In sum, and in view of the lack of a single prediction from the theory, we will eventually explore anxiety estimated both by ratings of manifest anxiety and by a speech-disturbance measure (Mahl, 1956), and relate these scores to measures of defense and cognitive style.

Although these operational inferences are not the only ones derivable from the theory, they are some of the main ones, and have been agreed to by other persons who are knowledgeable in psychoanalytic theory. At this point, however, they constitute only a partial base from which to evaluate the applicability of the theory of repression.

EVALUATION OF THE NEW FINDINGS

To review: A tape-recorded sample from 10 patients, each of whom experienced at least two instances of momentary forgetting, was assembled to try some of the hypotheses developed from the data of an earlier pilot study and from the concept of repression. Three areas were examined: cognitive disturbance; anxiety; relationship with the therapist. I was able to show that cognitive disturbance starts to build up about two minutes before the momentary forgetting and then subsides in about the same amount of time. Similarly, references to the therapist and high involvement with the therapist build up and decline within approximately the same period of time. Anxiety, at least as assessed by Mahl's (1956) speech-disturbance measure, shows no comparable build-up.

The patient who produced the most momentary forgetting was selected for a study of the consistency of theme. One main theme, rejection, was found across the 13 instances that occurred during the first 300 sessions. Other associated themes were involvement with the therapist, helplessness, and hostility. I should note here that the direction of the relationship between antecedent theme and the symptom is one-way: the emergence of a particular patient-specific theme is a *necessary* but *not sufficient* condition for momentary forgetting. Only rarely when the theme appears will momentary forgetting eventuate, but when momentary forgetting is present, this theme almost always precedes it. When this threatening theme is about to emerge, the patient can defend himself in a variety of ways. Forgetting is only one–and at that a rather infrequent–choice of symptom. Engel and Schmale (1967) note that this one-way quality is evident in the analysis of almost any symptom.

All in all, I have shown some lawfulness in a well-defined clinical phenomenon, and some tools for its analysis. Beyond that, there are only a few slender threads of inference consistent with a repression and transference interpretation; that is, the increase of cognitive disturbances and references to and involvement with the therapist. The demonstration of a recurrent threatening theme in the forgetting context within every patient, as shown in Patient X, would strengthen the strands of inference.

FROM HERE, WHERE?

I hope this report has given a sufficient sample of the reasoning, the tools, and the results. Many more inferences remain to be tested in these data. I will continue, and I hope others will as well. I am afraid that those who begin will falter on the laborious first step–collecting an adequate sample of forgettings and transcribing them. At the proper moment, therefore, I will share my data with anyone who has proper plans for replication or further exploration.

Future plans to carry the work further include testing more hypotheses suggested by the pilot work and by the present tape-recorded sample. That means scoring the present group of patients on a larger number of variables. The sample will be enlarged to a total of 15 patients who experience two or more instances of momentary forgetting plus at least five who show no momentary forgetting. The quality controls described earlier will be examined to see whether they affect any of the results. Thus, it will be possible to make a more systematic comparison between patients who show momentary forgetting and those who do not, and between those who show it frequently and those who show it rarely. We have arranged to obtain a psychological test battery on all patients, to inform us further about the nature of the patient population in the sample and the relationship of our findings to the personalities of the patients, especially the frequency of momentary forgetting and recovery versus nonrecovery of the forgotten thought.

Some of the work of scoring the large amount of material for some of the variables might be considerably eased by high involvement with a computer. From the research of Spence (1969a, 1969b) and Dahl (1972), computer dictionaries for some of the variables have been created. These will make it possible to compare a human-rating approach with a computer-counting approach, and may even eventuate in the rapid location of new discriminating variables.

As part of the further work to be done on assessing the development of anxiety that precedes momentary forgetting, we are considering the recording of physiological concomitants such as GSR and heart rate. The initiation of this work waits upon finding a patient who has a sufficiently high rate of momentary forgetting to make the investment in apparatus and recording worth while.

For the far distant future we envisage the development of methods of precipitating the memory disturbance through use of a drug or by some other manipulation such as hypnosis. It is conceivable that the manipulation will lower the threshold for such memory disturbances without materially altering some of the contexts ordinarily associated with momentary forgetting.

APPENDIX

EXAMPLES OF MOMENTARY FORGETTING: PATIENT X

Session 20

We couldn't continue treatment any more because, uh, because it wasn't doing me any good [4 sec.] or that you judge my, uh [3 sec.] my case to be not amenable to—to the treatment [4 sec.]. And I [3 sec.]–*I lost the other point that I, that I was about to* [4 sec.] *make*, after I tried to make, after I tried to explain why I wanted to make sure I didn't seem confused today [14 sec.]. For whatever reason the asso–the associated–the thing that flashed into my mind was a [hesitates]–was a scene with my mother [in which mother and sister "made fun of me and told me I was crazy"].

Session 36

. . . the business about, uh, "I present myself to you in such a way that I can't like you," whatever reasoning, uh, is behind that [2 sec.] that uh, nonsensical statement, uh [9 sec.] *Now I've lost the other thing that I was going to say* [7 sec.]. Oh [giggles] [sighs] now it's, it's so s–I mean it's silly, but I suppose [clears throat] it needs to be said, because it came to my mind, that, uh [4 sec.] that, uh, either on Monday, probably, I–hah [snort]–I became conscious, eh, uh, of these, I mean I her–a sound that I heard suggested that, uh, that you were, uh, brushing a spot off your, eh, off your trousers or something like, like your, uh, jacket sleeve, uh [3 sec.] and that I recall that while I was talking I had, I mean the fee–it–it struck me that you, uh, that you weren't really listening.

Session 53

. . . he hates his father, uh, and uh, trusts only his mother, sister, and godmother [2 sec.] and, uh [2 sec.] I mean I don't really think it applies to me, but somehow it's, uh, the fact that I thought it important to say that, but I [hesitates] don't know exactly why I thought it important. That is, it [hesitates] just seemed to me [hesitates] to suggest that, uh, all was not, uh, I mean to [2 sec.] to be further [3 sec.], uh, corroboration of–that's not the word I want–I mean–seems to fit into the picture of this, uh, of this boy's, uh, personality, as far as I could gather in a couple of hours [3 sec.] uh [6 sec.]. *I forgot now what I–what I had started to say just after that* [7 sec.]. Oh, well, one thing is that [hesitates] I did–I mean–I did feel a little, uh, frightened as I said, partly because of not being able to–uh, you know, I, it seemed–the minute I couldn't [2 sec.].– I couldn't understand, uh, a reaction of his. I [2 sec.]. I just–I mean–became almost mm–frozen 'cause–with fear, because I [hesitates] just felt I, eh [3 sec.] well, I don't know what I–I didn't–this didn't last long enough and I recognized it as uh [hesitates] as the same kind of, uh, feeling that I'd had [hesitates] when I couldn't understand why you did something. . . .

Session 66

. . . it wasn't because of what I'd been saying, uh, we j–we just had to stop because the time was up. In other words, that you–I mean, that was kind of you and uh [15 sec.] I–*there was something else that I was leading up to, and I seem to have lost it* [25 sec.]. Oh, then I um, somehow, um, last night I started thinking again about uh, about the summer [4 sec.] [clears throat] appearing as if I would uh, I ss–It's partly [4 sec.]–I mean, for what–whatever this, uh, the analyzable roots of it are, I feel as if [4 sec.] as if I want to uh, to do something to uh, bear witness to uh, certain things that I think that I feel, and so that I would like to uh, to perhaps, if–if it all worked out uh, to go and teach, or work in a community center somewhere in the South for at least a month in the summer . . . [and wants Therapist's O.K. for the time off].

Session 83

. . . I would be hurt [i.e., if Therapist forgot the session] but uh, I'd get over it [1 min. 48 sec.]. There was a–I was–I did–when I was thinking about uh, uh, what I uh, do feel about you [4 sec.] well, I su–I mean my feelings are ones of uh, affection and uh [6 sec.] and I think confidence–I mean, yes, confidence–I don't have to put "I think" in there uh [7 sec.]. *What I was going to say slipped out of my head* [sigh]. [Therapist: I–I didn't hear that.] I said w–I was going on to say something else, uh. [Therapist: That you suddenly forgot?] Yes [4 sec.] well maybe this wi–will throw some light on it, I mean, just by virtue of association. It isn't what I was going to say but [3 sec.] but uh, it occurred to me to wonder whether [hesitates] that time, a couple weeks ago when I uh, cried so bitterly because uh, I thought everything was all over uh, you seemed to–to think that it uh, it was because I was so uh [hesitates] shocked, and felt rejected that [2 sec.] that uh [3 sec.], that Monday hour hadn't been a full hour. And I won–wonder, I don't know, this may be just a way of avoiding the notion that I do have real feelings for you.

Session 91

I said I seemed very nicely to have picked on men–who either intentionally or unintentionally uh, and then I meant to say, "don't treat me well," and I [2 sec.] then a phrase fla–flashed through my mind [hesitates] "get in my way" [exhales] [12 sec.]. *Now I don't know what else I was going to say* [4 sec.]. [Therapist: You mean you forgot for a moment?] Yes. [2 sec.] I mean that was just preparatory to saying the–that thing–for the phrase, "get in my way," uh, flashed across my mind as I was [2 sec.] trying to get to the sentence I intended to say [7 sec.] [exhales]. Oh [snort] uh, I just was–I mean I–I was going–I was saying that the feeling is [6 sec.] is uh, to a degree, justified, except that I do the choosing of the men. . . .

3

BRAIN WAVE CORRELATES OF SUBLIMINAL STIMULATION, UNCONSCIOUS ATTENTION, PRIMARY- AND SECONDARY-PROCESS THINKING, AND REPRESSIVENESS

HOWARD SHEVRIN

In this paper I will describe a series of experiments which show, for the first time to my knowledge, a relationship between the electrical activity of the brain in response to a stimulus and unconscious thought processes involving attention, perception, primary-process thinking, and repression. Not all of the findings are solidly established, but the experimental method is rich in possibilities for investigating complex psychological events of interest to the psychoanalyst. This method draws upon two techniques, subliminal stimulation and the cortical evoked response, which will now be described.

SUBLIMINAL STIMULATION

Experimental work on subliminal stimulation goes back to well before the turn of the century, but it was not until Fisher (1956; Fisher and Paul, 1959) undertook to replicate Pötzl's lit-

The research reported in this chapter has been supported by National Institute of Mental Health Grant Nos. M-2257, MH-18719, and GRS FR-05517-06, by the Pfeiffer Foundation, and by the Research Department of the Menninger Foundation. The early phases of the research dealing with the rebus technique were enriched by the collaborative contributions of Drs. Lester Luborsky, Lawrence Stross, and Charles Fisher. Subsequent work dealing with the evoked response measures has benefited from the contributions of Dr. William H. Smith, Dr. Philip Rennick, and Mr. Dean E. Fritzler, Mr. Benjamin Naylor and Mr. Ray Hoobler assisted in the execution of the experiments and data reduction. Mr. Rex Hartzell, Head, Biomedical Electronics Laboratory, and members of his staff provided invaluable assistance by maintaining in good functioning order the complex electronic equipment necessary for the research. Miss Lolafaye Coyne, Chief Statistician, supervised most of the analyses reported in this chapter.

tle-known tachistoscopic experiments that investigations of subliminal stimulation were made relevant to psychoanalysis. Over the past 15 years more such studies have steadily accumulated, accompanied by heated controversy. Out of this controversy the existence of subliminal perception has emerged as a new scientific fact. This conclusion was reached by Bevan (1964), an entirely nonanalytically oriented psychologist and an accomplished experimentalist, on the basis of his review of over 80 studies.[1] In all the sound and fury of debate about the status of psychoanalytic concepts, the quiet birth of this scientific fact bearing so direct a relationship to psychoanalysis, born in the laboratory and not in the consulting room, has gone unnoticed. The baby is thriving, and as one of the first legitimate offsprings of psychoanalysis and experimental psychology it deserves some special consideration.

The center of interest can now shift from demonstrating the existence of subliminal perception to exploring its nature. Here we can expect new controversy. Bevan, although conceding the existence of subliminal perception, does not believe that the evidence warrants the conclusion that subliminal input is subject to laws of perception and association different from those governing supraliminal perception. Klein (1959) and Gill (1963), from the perspective of ego psychology, have also interpreted the data as suggesting that subliminal input is generally subject to a nondynamic inhibition rather than to a repressive force which would result in primary-process distortions in thinking. Elsewhere I have argued (Shevrin, 1968) that this interpretation can be challenged, in the light of the available evidence and because of the limited place accorded motives and transference factors in most subliminal experiments.

In the subliminal method used in the work to be described, a special stimulus was constructed which is capable of eliciting several types of associations related to the psychoanalytic distinc-

[1] In a more recent comprehensive review and analysis of research on subliminal perception, Dixon (1971) concluded that the existence of subliminal perception has been demonstrated in at least eight different contexts: dreams, memory, adaptation level, conscious perception, verbal behavior, emotional responses, drive-related behavior, and perceptual thresholds.

tions between primary- and secondary-process thinking. The aim was to investigate the conditions under which a subliminal input would undergo primary- and secondary-process transformations in the associative process. The method draws on certain psychoanalytic assumptions about language and speech in dream, symptom formation, and psychosis. We assume, for example, that in dream formation words may be treated as clanglike auditory patterns, seeming to lose their conceptual function. It is further assumed that this loss of conceptual function occurs as part of the defensive displacement and condensing process of dream work. An especially rich illustration of this process can be found in Erikson's (1954) description of a dream that consisted of one word, SEINE, in which was compounded allusions to the French river, the Latin word SINE, the English word SIN, and the German words SEHN and SEINE. Words can be pivotal in the formation of a dream; they have the further advantage for the experimenter of being easy units to identify and to add up in various ways for purposes of measurement. For technical reasons, however, it is advisable for the stimuli themselves not to be words, but to be capable of eliciting words. One such technical reason is that words, being greatly overlearned, have remarkably low recognition thresholds. It is also important that the elements of the stimulus should not ordinarily occur together. Most ordinary pictures, for example, have a great deal of internal consistency. A picture of a street scene would be a poor stimulus because if one were to catch a glimpse of a house such associations as street, tree, car, etc., would naturally follow and would not be instances of true subliminal perception. A stimulus constructed to overcome these problems is illustrated in Figure 1. It is a picture of a pen and a knee. Pens and knees do not ordinarily occur together and thus have a low order of contingent association. If one were to think of pen it is highly unlikely that one would also think of knee, and vice versa. The picture is of much more than a pen and a knee—there is a leg, calf, thigh, pen point, etc. It is also a male phallic symbol and a female knee; it is also cut off, mutilated, and contains hostile as well as sexual connotations. For present purposes, however, these other factors have been ignored (but it is by no means denied that all of these may play some part in subliminal perception). Instead, our interest has

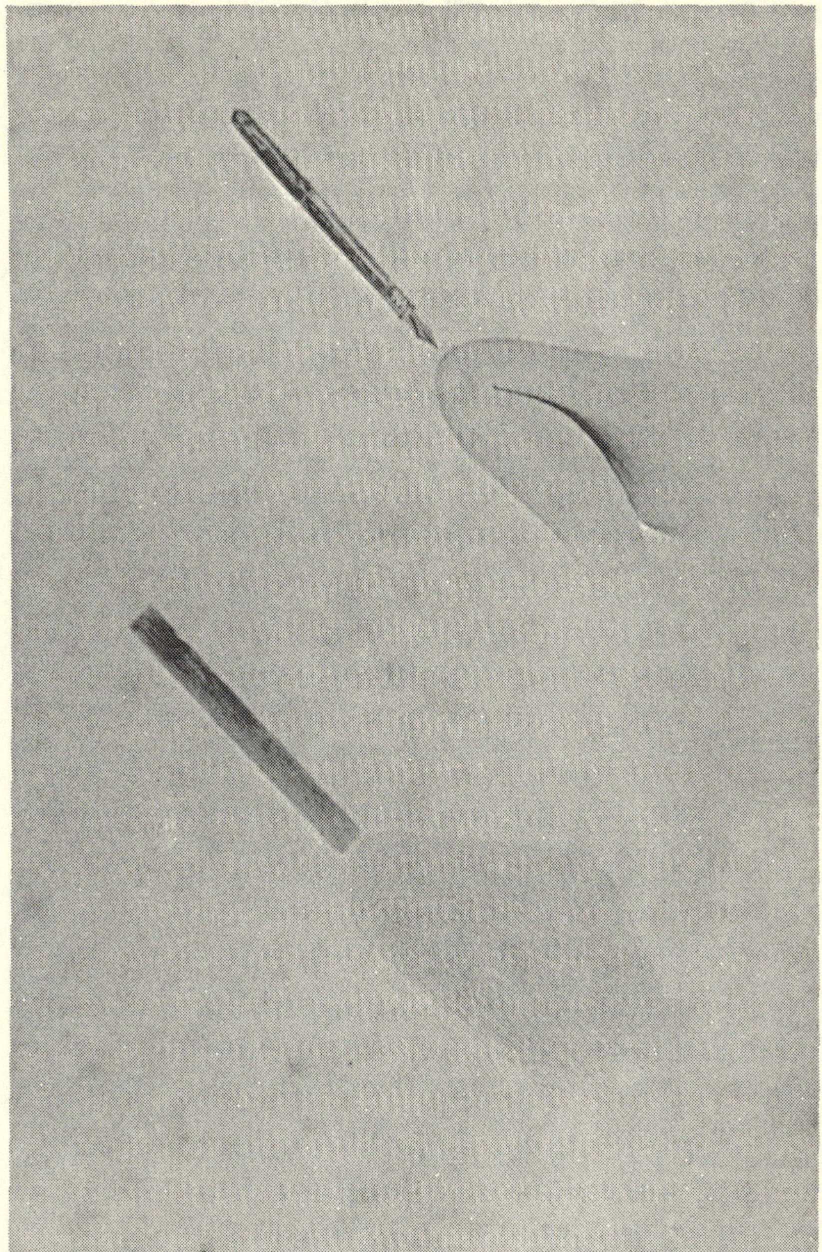

FIGURE 1. Experimental stimuli. The PEN/KNEE is the rebus (R) stimulus. Lower stimulus is abstract (D) stimulus. The actual stimuli are in color: the pen is dark gray with a gold nib, the knee is a light flesh tone.

been focused on certain verbal relationships and transformations. The two objects can be designated as a pen and a knee with the customary dictionary meanings of the words in mind. These words, however, can be treated in the associative process as concepts, clangs, or clang combinations. Thus, when they are treated as concepts, associations such as *ink*, *paper*, and *write* to pen, and *leg*, *calf*, and *body* to knee, may occur. When, however, they are treated as clangs, associations such as *pen*nant or hap*pen*, or *ne*ither or a*ny* may occur. Lastly, the words can be combined or "condensed" to form a new word, *penny*, totally unrelated in meaning to the objects themselves. This clang combination in turn may give rise to associations–*coin*, *round*, *poor*, etc. By obtaining association norms for these key words it is possible to score these association effects with a degree of reliability limited only by scoring error, which has generally been less than 3%. The conceptual associations, based on words referring to objects, are close to the secondary process, whereas the clang and clang-combination associations, based on words treated as "things" or auditory patterns, are close to the primary process. The stimulus is a rebus–a pictorial representation of a word; it is a little waking fragment of what we suspect happens on a grander scale in the formation of a dream. The three levels of association will be designated as *conceptual*, *clang*, and *rebus*.

A series of studies has been carried out with the PEN/KNEE rebus and other rebuses. In general, the findings are encouraging. With earlier versions of two rebuses (TIE/KNEE and BEE/GUN), we found that rebuses exposed subliminally can influence word choices in the expected direction (Shevrin and Luborsky, 1961). Moreover, at prolonged supraliminal exposures subjects could not identify the rebus level without broad hints, although many had already responded at this level following a previous subliminal exposure. This finding was interpreted to mean that primary-process thinking is not easily accessible in the usual alert, conscious, waking state. In another study in which the rebus method was used, we were able to show that the same subliminal input can enter into sleep consciousness in significantly different ways (Shevrin and Fisher, 1967). We found that penny associates were more numerous in associations following REM awakenings, and that pen and knee associations were more numerous in associations following NREM awakenings. Both types of association occurred with greater frequency following their respective sleep stages than in the presleep waking state (see Figure 2). We interpreted these findings as showing

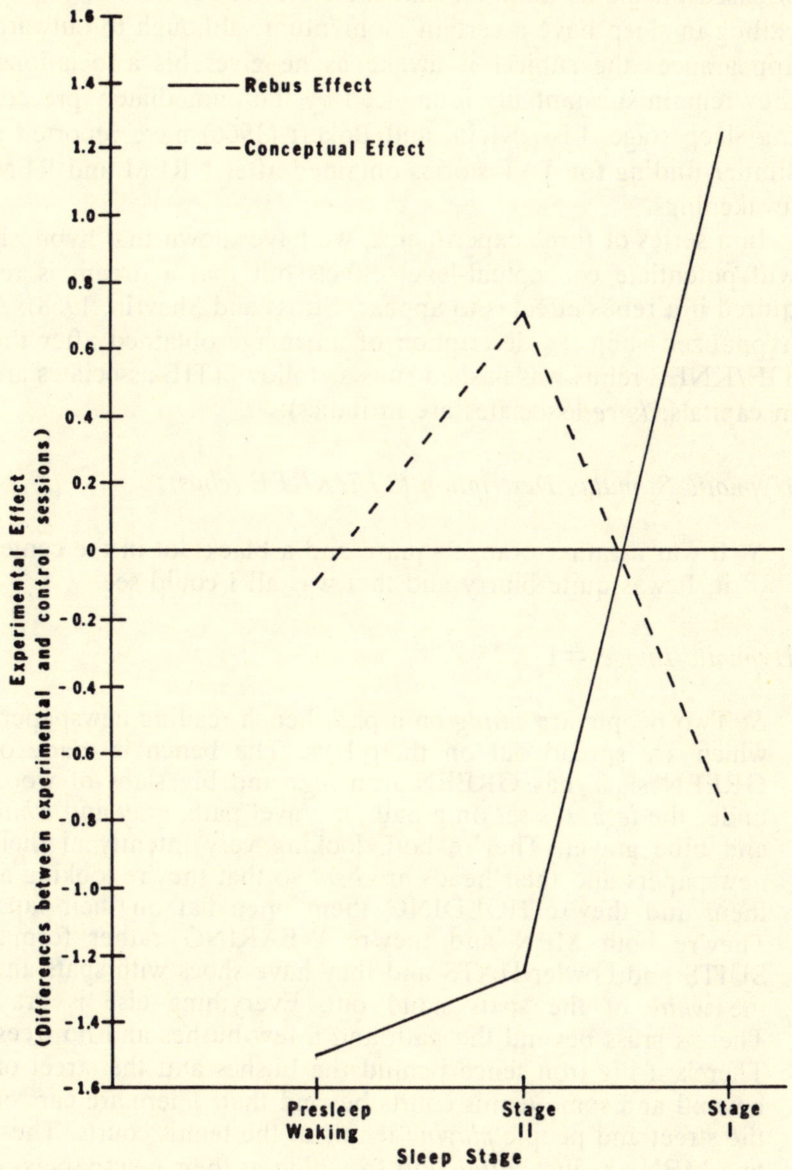

FIGURE 2. Rebus and conceptual subliminal effects as a function of sleep stages. (Median values; N = 10.)

that the primary-process reworking of a subliminal input occurred in REM sleep and that the secondary-process reworking of the same input occurred in NREM sleep. This interpretation is based on the assumption that the states of consciousness prevailing in sleep have a certain momentum: although to outward appearances the subject is awake as he gives his associations, they remain substantially influenced by the immediately preceding sleep stage. Fiss, Klein, and Bokert (1966) have reported a similar finding for TAT stories obtained after NREM and REM awakenings.

In a series of three experiments, we have shown that hypnosis will potentiate conceptual-level effects but that a dream is required if a rebus effect is to appear (Stross and Shevrin, 1968). A hypnotized subject's description of an image obtained after the TIE/KNEE rebus was flashed runs as follows (TIE associates are in capitals; *knee* associates are in italics):

Hypnotic Stimulus Description (TIE/KNEE rebus)

S: It was a rather orange square and a black dot in the center of it. It was quite blurry and that was all I could see.

Hypnotic Image #1

S: Two people are *sitting* on a park bench reading newspapers which are spread out on their laps. The bench is made of GREEN slats, has GREEN iron *legs* and big slabs of wood under the *legs*. It's set on a path, a gravel path, gray and *white* and blue gravel. They're both looking very intently at their newspapers and their heads are *bent* so that they're looking at them and they're HOLDING them open flat on their laps. They're both MEN and they're WEARING rather formal SUITS and bowler HATS and they have shoes with spats and the *white* of the spats stand out. Everything else is gray. There's grass beyond the path and a few bushes and no trees. There's a big iron fence behind the bushes and the street on beyond and some tennis courts beyond that. There are cars on the street and people *playing* tennis at the tennis courts. These two MEN are just *sitting* and frowning at their newspapers.

A hypnotized subject's recall of a dream obtained the day after the PEN/KNEE rebus was flashed reads as follows (*penny* associates are in italics):

Hypnotic Stimulus Description (PEN/KNEE rebus)

> *S*: It just looked like a couple of broad lines that moved horizontally across the picture. The top line being, sloping upward.

Hypnotic Dream Recall

> *S*: I was carrying this suitcase and a violin and a bunch of other packages and I told her I been, just arrived in town from out of town. I had just traveled and I was just worn out so she apologized and got a colored lady from the ladies' room to come and help me and this lady was very help–, very kind but she picked up all, just a few of these little packages [laughs], the luggage and the violin and I took them out through the department *store* out to a lawn where we were, this *friend* then was out there waiting for a taxicab and she had other luggage there. I put down my packages there but this time the colored lady had taken these little parcels into the washroom and I had to go back after her and get them and come back to where the taxicab and luggage was and then I was confused because I didn't know how much to tip the porter that was putting our baggage in the taxicab and this *girl* who had helped and I finally decided I'd tip them both the same. I gave them a *quarter* and a *dime* and she was pleased because I had, she had felt I had tipped her quite a bit, rather tipped her as much as I had the man who had done much more.

On the assumption that the hypnotic state would be sensitive to primary-process thinking, we had hypothesized that hypnosis would augment both rebus and clang effects. We found, however, that dream work is necessary before these primary-process effects can appear. On the basis of clinical and theoretical considerations, Brenman (1949) reached a similar conclusion. The findings from these various studies demonstrate that the rebus method works and can bring some interesting relationships to light.

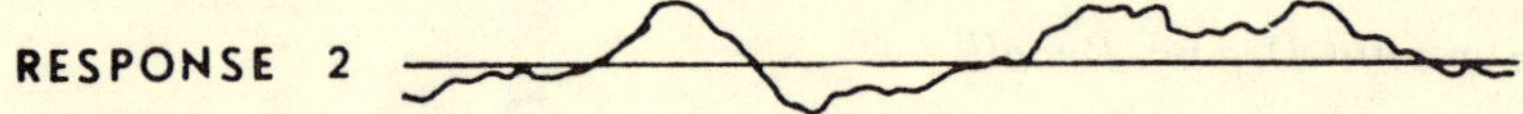

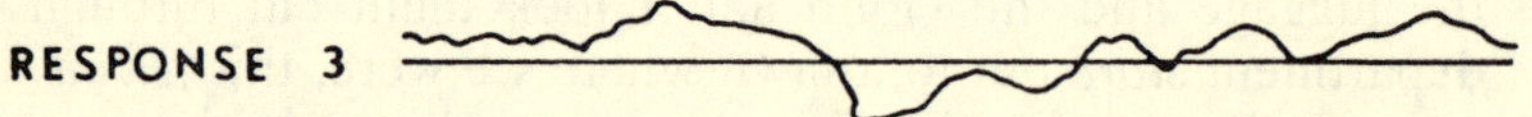

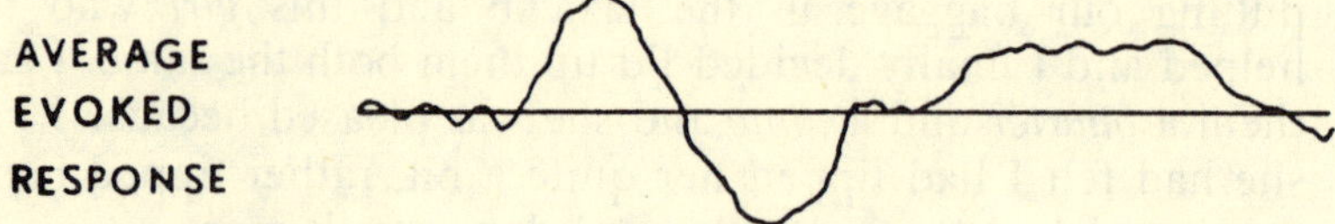

SCHEMATIC REPRESENTATION OF AVERAGING METHOD

FIGURE 3. Responses 1, 2, and 3 represent samples of EEG-recorded brain responses obtained immediately after a given stimulus has been presented. The bottom curve is the *average* of these three curves, showing how a component recurring in response to a stimulus will be clearly visible whereas random activity or noise will tend to "average out."

CORTICAL EVOKED RESPONSES

The second method on which the research is based is the average evoked response, or AER. Until this method was devised it was extremely difficult to detect the brain's response to a discrete stimulus. The EEG itself is a melange of interacting responses to a great variety of internal and external stimuli, and can show a discriminating response only if amplitudes are substantially high. With a small-sized computer, however, it is possible to "feed in" EEG data and to obtain in return a response pattern in the form of a curve which shows the brain's specific response to a discontinuous repetitive stimulus in any modality. Figure 3 shows schematically how this averaging is accomplished. In the upper three curves are the "raw" EEG responses to a given stimulus. One component, varying in amplitude and slightly in latency, is present in each curve. Much of the remaining activity varies considerably from response to response. The common wave component will remain in the final average curve (see bottom line of Figure 3), while the randomly varying waves will tend to cancel each other out. The common wave component thus represents the brain's specific response to a stimulus.

The new technique is based on one of the oldest scientific methods–what J. S. Mill referred to as the method of concomitant variation. In more modern terms, the signal-to-noise ratio is increased, so that the signal–the stimulus-related activity–can be detected, while the "noise"–the stimulus-irrelevant activity–is appreciably reduced. The signal which emerges has one intriguing property–it seems to be associated with attention. For example, if a subject is instructed to attend to *dim* flashes interspersed among bright flashes, the amplitude of the average evoked response within approximately the first 260 msec. will be greater for the dim flashes than for the bright flashes (Haider, Spong, and Lindsley, 1964). Intuitively, we would expect the bright flashes to induce a bigger wave; that is not what happens, however, because the amplitude is not a simple function of intensity but is also associated with a complex psychological event–attention. In a review of some 162 studies, Tecce (1970) concluded that the preponderance of the evidence favors the hypothesis that certain components that appear within 200–300 msec. poststimulus are concomitants of attention, although considerably more work in clarifying certain variables needs to be done. From a psychological and psychoanalytic point of view, this is an exciting discovery: a complex psychological event like attention has been found to have a specific brain referent. Moreover, the method is objective and not difficult to master. A good deal of recent work (Donchin and Lindsley, 1969) shows that muscle artifacts cannot account for these waves and–more important–that there is a close morphological similarity between the evoked responses obtained with scalp electrodes and those obtained with implanted electrodes. It is doubtful that we are dealing with artifactual responses produced by muscle potentials, by interference from the skull and scalp, or by pupillary changes.

A series of experiments will now be described in which the subliminal and evoked response methods were combined.

The First Study: Cortical Response to a Tactile Stimulus during Attention, Mental Arithmetic, and Free Associations (Shevrin and Rennick, 1967). This experiment is in some respects a "warm-up." We wanted to see for ourselves whether the average evoked response was associated with attention, as others had reported. In addition, we wanted to find out (a) if the evoked response could be used to discriminate between different concomitant psychological processes, and (b) if the evoked response would vary with the effects of a subliminal stimulus. The latter question was in this experiment a secondary one.

The stimulus was a light touch to the index finger delivered by a delicately balanced stylus some 40 times at intervals ranging from two to six seconds. Subjects were asked to perform three tasks: selective attention, mental arithmetic, and free association. In selective attention, the subject was asked to pay careful attention to the stimuli and to estimate the varying time intervals between successive touches. In mental arithmetic, the subject was asked to subtract serially by sevens from some randomly selected high number (320, 410, etc.) while the tactile stimulus was being delivered. In free association, the subject was asked to let individual words come to mind for a period of two minutes while the tactile stimulus was being delivered. Each set was induced twice in a counterbalanced order. The electrode placement was bipolar: parietal-frontal. Before "hooking up" the subject, we flashed the picture of either a pen or a knee at 1 msec. The pen was flashed for one group of subjects, and the knee for another group. The subliminal part of this experiment was secondary but nevertheless of interest. The rebus picture was split up to provide a control for other experiments: to see if rebus effects would appear even if the rebus segments were not combined. We found no such rebus effects. The influence of the two subliminal stimuli was to be detected in the free associations. The subjects were 12 pairs of twins, ranging in age from 13 to 19, borrowed from Gardner's (1964) longitudinal study of cognitive styles and defenses in twins. The reason for using twins will become apparent later.

Our hypotheses in this study were:

1. If the average evoked response is related to attention, certain amplitudes should be greater in selective attention than in either mental arithmetic or free association. These latter two tasks were in effect distracting conditions.

2. If the average evoked response can subtly reflect differences in concomitant psychological processes, then the average evoked responses for mental arithmetic and free association should differ.

From a psychological standpoint, mental arithmetic is decidedly different from free associating. Mental arithmetic requires the subject to concentrate on a pattern of mental manipulations, whereas free associating requires the opposite–attention to internal processes but no manipulation of them.

3. If the average evoked response is associated with attention and thus can reflect a shift between inwardly and outwardly directed attention, then the evoked response components associated with attention to the *external* tactile stimulus should be lower for subjects who show high sensitivity to the subliminal stimulus in their free associations. Here we are assuming that the subliminal stimulus evokes associations which become conscious in greater numbers if attention is directed to internal cues.

The findings are schematically represented in Figure 4. The first hypothesis was confirmed. The trough-to-peak amplitude, A–B, which peaks at approximately 107 msec., was greater in selective attention than in free association or mental arithmetic. Also, the two amplitudes measured from baseline to peak, B and D, were significantly greater in selective attention than in the

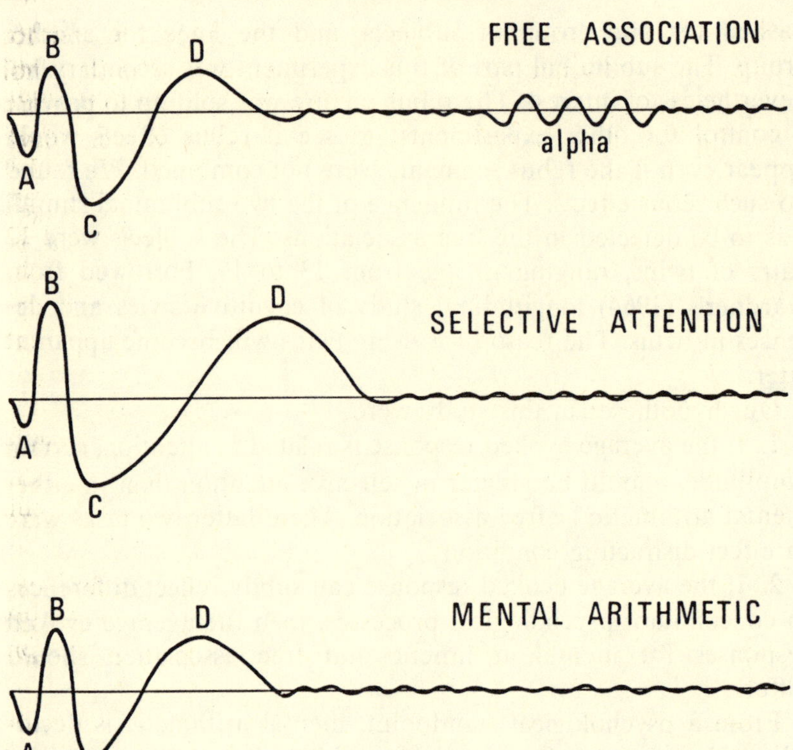

FIGURE 4. Curves represent typical conformations for each condition. Amplitudes and latencies at points A, B, C, and D were computed from the average of 48 measurements made in each condition. Incidence of α bursts is indicated schematically.

TABLE 1

AMPLITUDES OF AER COMPONENTS MEASURED FROM ESTIMATED BASELINE (WITH LAST 500 MSEC. OF 2-SEC. READOUT USED TO DRAW BASELINE THROUGH FIRST 1000 MSEC.)

Condition	A wave	B wave	A to b (trough to peak)	C wave	D wave
Free association	3.90	−4.52 $>p<.001$	8.43 $>p<.05$	7.71	−3.76 $>p<.01$
Selective attention	2.81	−8.54 $>p<.01$	11.38 $>p<.05$	8.23	−6.99 $>p<.05$
Mental arithmetic	3.74	−5.54	9.28	6.86	−4.77

The trough-to-peak amplitudes computed from point A to point B are included to provide a measure independent of errors in estimating the baseline. Significance levels less than .05 are shown.

other two conditions. A summary of these findings is presented in Table 1. The latency of peak D occurred significantly later in selective attention than in free association or mental arithmetic (670 msec. versus 492 msec. and 489 msec. respectively, $p < .01$ for both comparisons). In Figure 5 a set of actual curves from one subject is shown. In the second free-association curve there is a burst of alpha (synchronized brain activity in the 8–12 per second range) which is not found in any of the selective-attention or mental-arithmetic curves. The presence of alpha in free association significantly discriminated free-association curves from either the selective-attention or mental-arithmetic curves (χ^2 for correlated proportions $= 9.00$, $p = .004$). The second hypothesis was to some degree supported in an interesting and unexpected way. The average evoked response did reveal a difference between free association and mental arithmetic in one particular parameter, alpha, often associated with drowsy, distracted states. Alpha is inhibited by problem solving and by attention to an external stimulus.

Lastly, we found that among the 12 subjects shown the pen stimulus there was a fortuitous split (six and six) between subjects who used pen associates and those who used none at all. When we compared these two subgroups we found that the B amplitude (the electrically negative portion of the A–B component) was *less* than half as great in the subjects who showed a subliminal effect as it was in the subjects who showed no subliminal effect (3.50 versus 7.22, $t = 2.287$, $p < .05$). A comparable effect could not be shown for the subjects shown the knee stimulus. The finding was thus limited to one of the two subliminal stimuli. For the pen stimulus it seemed that an inverse relationship existed between directing attention outward (to the tactile stimulus) and directing attention inward (to associations related to the subliminal stimulus). This finding is consistent with Rapaport's (1959b) assumption that attention is available only in a determinate quantity in a given state so that there is "competition for it . . . between internal and external excitations" (p. 782).

This first experiment was encouraging. The average evoked response was not only associated with attention but could reflect differences in psychological states, as well as *shifts* in attention with respect to a subliminal stimulus. One could be emboldened

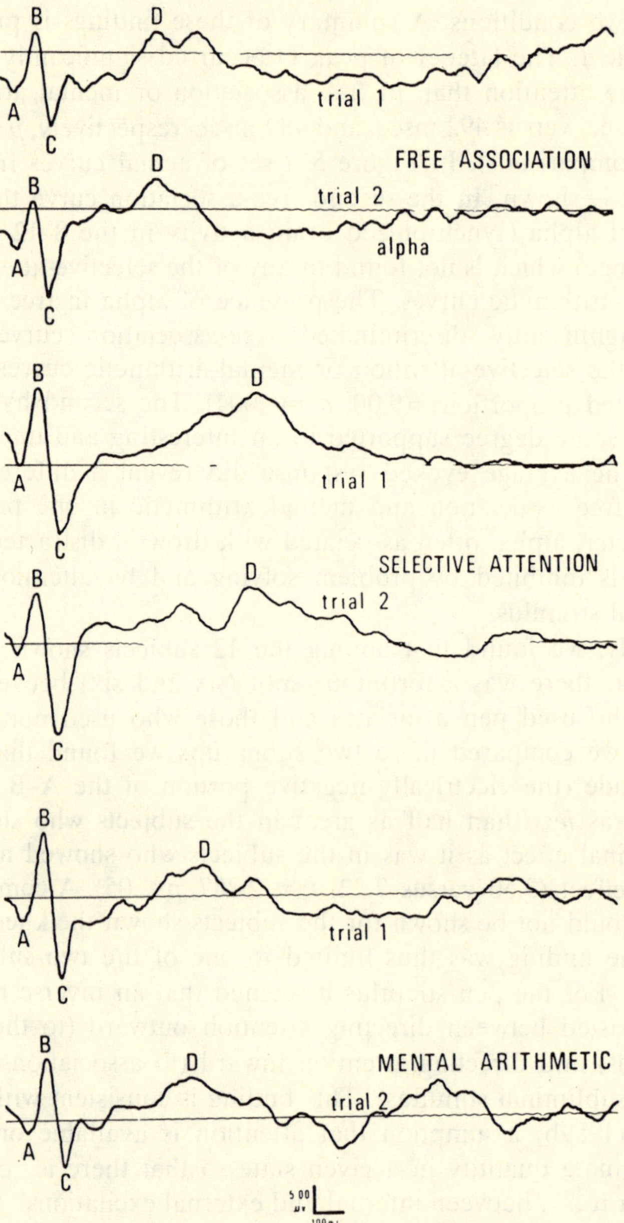

FIGURE 5. Set of 6 AER curves obtained from Subject A, 13-year-old male fraternal twin; each curve is based on 40 sweeps. Points A, B, C, and D mark peak amplitudes analyzed in study. Incidence of α bursts noted wherever present during last 1,000 msec. Baseline estimated from last 500 msec. of record.

to inquire if average evoked responses might reveal the presence of a brain response to a subliminal stimulus.

The Second Study: Visual Evoked Response Correlates of Unconscious Mental Processes (Shevrin and Fritzler, 1968a). This experiment was appealing not only because of empirical considerations but also because of an important theoretical consideration. Elsewhere I have hypothesized that the existence of subliminal perception forces us to assume that attention can be unconscious, and that a concept of neutral registration which does not involve attention and motivation is untenable (Shevrin, 1968). It was argued that perception implies attention, whether it be conscious, preconscious, or unconscious. No perceptual process is possible without a prior and concomitant act of attention. From this point of view, the "sense-organ" concept of consciousness as dispensing or withholding attention is too limited. Incongruous as it sounds, attention can be dispensed unconsciously as well, but the idea is no more incongruous than that of unconscious perception itself. In a posthumously published paper, Rapaport suggested something quite similar: "Nothing can be perceived–whether such perception is indicated by the consensually validated consciousness of the perceived or by the symptoms consisting of impingements upon other cognitive experiences–without its being so hypercathected. Thus *attention cathecting does not per se guarantee consciousness* or the form of conscious appearance of the internal or external excitation" (1959b, p. 781; italics added). Subliminal perception would be one class of perceptions whose presence is revealed by "impingements upon other cognitive experiences" and as such has been cathected with attention but has not become conscious.

The fact that the evoked response is associated with attention thus provides a means for testing this theoretical construction concerning unconscious attention. If the idea is valid, the average evoked response should show an increase in amplitude associated with attention whenever a subliminal stimulus had been attended to unconsciously. Furthermore, if we are dealing with something beyond a primitive sensing process, such as an orienting response, we should be able to find associates to the subliminal stimulus in free associations. If both hypotheses are

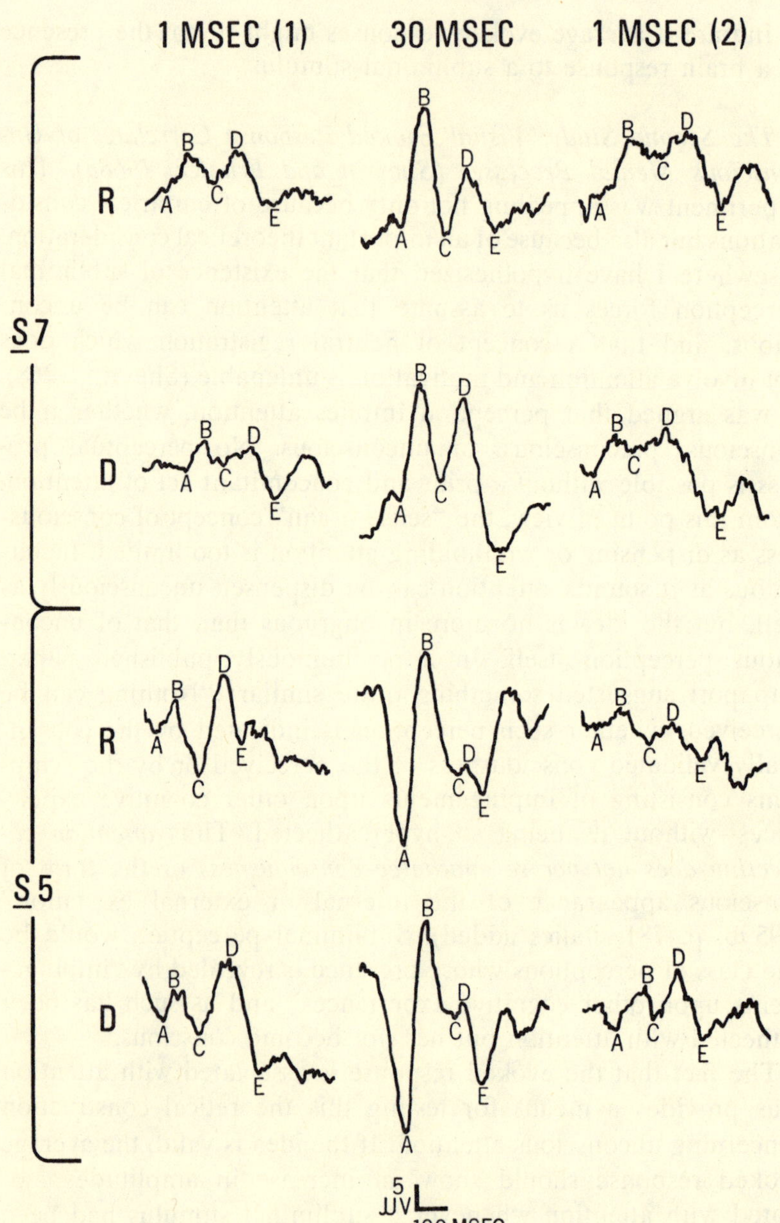

FIGURE 6. Average evoked responses (from Subjects 7 and 5 drawn from study by Shevrin and Fritzler, 1968a) as recorded from frontal-occipital electrodes for each exposure condition and for each stimulus, R and D. Average evoked responses are based on approximately 30 sweeps for each curve. Positive polarity downward.

confirmed, it could then be argued that the average evoked response is associated with an unconscious act of attention and perception which represents the starting point of an unconscious thought process revealed in free associations.

In order to make the test as rigorous as possible, the average evoked response technique was given the task of discriminating between two stimuli matched for size, color, general configuration, and brightness, but differing in specific content (Figure 1 above). In this respect the procedure was different from that of Libet et al. (1967), who found average evoked response correlates for somatosensory stimuli of subthreshold *intensity.* Our interest was in the *content* and *quality* of thought processes. Pribram, Spinelli, and Kamback (1967), working with monkeys, had already reported that average evoked responses could discriminate between a circle and striations, each presented for 1 msec. In our study, the two stimuli were presented for 1 msec., for 30 msec., and again for 1 msec. In each condition the PEN/KNEE rebus (Stimulus R) was flashed for a total of 30 times and its matched control (Stimulus D) 30 times in a modified random order. Between blocks of 10 stimulations–5 Rs and 5 Ds–free associations of 2 minutes' duration were obtained for a total of 12 minutes for each of the three conditions. The two stimuli were both flashed within one block in order to control for possible habituation effects. Since the main purpose of the experiment was to see if a brain discrimination could be found, we were ready to sacrifice to some extent the possibility of establishing verbal effects, for both stimuli would have been flashed before obtaining each series of free associations. As will be shown later, however, it is possible to identify some subliminal verbal effects in this experiment, and we have in subsequent work established verbal effects following the *separate* flashing of the rebus and control stimuli. At 1 msec. subjects saw nothing of the stimulus; at 30 msec. they could distinguish between the two stimuli, although they still found it difficult to recognize them. The subjects were 11 male undergraduates. The electrode display was bipolar: frontal-occipital. The occipital electrode was placed 2 cm. to the left above the inion. The frontal electrode was placed close to the hairline at the midline.

We found that the average evoked response discriminated

between the stimuli with equal effectiveness whether the stimuli were subliminal or supraliminal, although the effect was strongest in the first 1 msec. condition ($F = 11.58$, 1/10 df, $p < .01$). Moreover, the main discriminating component was within the poststimulus time interval associated with attention in other studies (approximately 250–300 msec.). Average evoked responses for two subjects are shown in Figure 6. The main discriminating component is the positive-going amplitude from B–C.

Both rebus and conceptual verbal effects were found in the free associations for the first 1 msec. condition on the basis of the following method: the approach to measuring subliminal verbal effects was developed in a series of other studies in which it was found that more associates appeared to a stimulus which was not consciously discriminated than to the same stimulus when it was consciously discriminated (Shevrin and Luborsky, 1958, 1961; Spence, 1964; Spence and Holland, 1962). Spence has referred to this factor as the "restrictive effects of awareness." On the basis of these findings, we hypothesized that more associates would be given following the 1 msec. stimulus exposures than following the 30 msec. exposures. This comparison of verbal effects following two exposure conditions was made necessary by the fact that both stimuli (R and D) as mentioned previously were flashed within each block of trials before free associations were obtained. Both stimuli were presented within the same block in order to maximize AER discrimination between the two stimuli by minimizing habituation effects. When this method was used we found that there were significantly more knee and penny associates in the first 1 msec. condition than in the 30 msec. condition (Friedman Test, $p < .01$, knee associates; $p < .05$, penny associates).

For the first time to my knowledge, both electrocortical and linguistic effects from a subliminal stimulus had been obtained. Would there be any correlation between these two seemingly diverse indices? We found that the incidence of conceptual associates was positively correlated with both the B–C amplitudes for R and D for the first 1 msec. condition. The best estimate of both indices was provided by a combined conceptual effect (pen and knee associates) and a combined R and D amplitude score. The resulting rank-order correlation was .70 ($p < .05$). Neither rebus nor clang effect was significantly correlated with amplitude. However, when the incidence of alphalike activity approximately 1.5 seconds poststimulus (comparable to the alpha found in the first study) was measured, it correlated significantly with both rebus and clang effects (.75, $p < .01$, and .73, $p < .02$, respectively). The correlations with the conceptual effects were now nonsignificant. It would appear that the parameter of the average evoked response associated with attention is also associated with a secondary-process subliminal effect, while another average evoked response parameter, alpha, is associated with a primary-process subliminal effect. The fact that these findings are present for both the R and D responses suggested that we may be dealing with a stable *state* rather than with specific transient effects.

The Third Study: Average Evoked Response and Verbal Correlates of Unconscious Mental Processes (Shevrin, Smith, and Fritzler, 1971). In this replication a number of refinements in measuring average evoked responses were introduced. The subjects were again 12 pairs of twins, a choice which was especially useful for the investigation of repressiveness to be described below. The main findings from this study confirmed what had been previously found. Moreover, this time all effects were specifically linked to stimulus R: (1) the B–C amplitude was significantly greater for Stimulus R than for Stimulus D in the first 1 msec. condition and in the 30 msec. condition; this difference was found on the basis of two different criteria for identifying the B–C amplitude, described in detail elsewhere (Shevrin, Smith, and Fritzler, 1971) (sequence method: $F = 6.033$, 1/10 *df*, $p < .05$; peak amplitude method: $F = 10.477$, 1/10 *df*, $p < .01$); (2) knee associates were significantly more numerous in the first 1 msec. condition than in the 30 msec. condition (Friedman Test, $p < .05$); (3) the incidence of knee associates was a function of the B–C amplitude for Stimulus R only (sequence method, Wilcoxon Signed Rank Test, $p < .05$); (4) the incidence of penny associates was a function of alpha for Stimulus R only.

RELATIONSHIPS WITH REPRESSIVENESS

From a metapsychological point of view my references to unconscious thought processes have been equivocal. It would be more correct to say that the electrocortical and verbal effects thus far described are *descriptively*, rather than *dynamically*, unconscious. We do not know as yet if we are dealing with dynamically unconscious processes. The evidence that rebus effects are present does suggest that primary-process transformations of a sort associated with dynamic unconscious phenomena occur. However, there is no direct evidence of the kind of defensive activity associated with dynamically unconscious processes. Defensive activity might well be influencing the evoked response and subliminal effects, but we have no independent assessment of its presence. If we infer from the existence of clang and rebus effects both the existence of primary-process thinking and the operation of defenses, we are in danger of circularity.

However, there is a way in which an independent assessment of defensive activity can be made, although the approach still remains at some distance from the actual focus of such activity. I refer to the clinical assessment of defenses on the basis of psychological tests. At the heart of this diagnostic assessment are certain assumptions about the long-term effects of a defense upon thinking, reality testing, and character formation. For instance, a person who relies mainly on repression will show a pervasive lack of interest in ideation, know less about the world then his general level of intelligence would lead one to expect, and show a readiness to respond overemotionally to circumstances. When we have evidence for these traits on psychological tests we infer that the person characteristically relies on repression as a defense. It is important to stress that rarely do we have direct evidence of actual repression, that is, individual instances of repression. In effect, we make the inference on the basis of a probability model: given these characteristics, it is highly likely that the person relies on repression more often than on other defenses and more often than do people who are dissimilar in these respects. For this reason it is better to talk about *repressiveness*, that is, a *tendency* to repress, than about repression, that is, actual instances of repression. This is in principle no different from what any experienced clinician does in the course of a clinical examination. Tests make it easier to compare different people because they are administered and scored in a uniform and systematic manner.

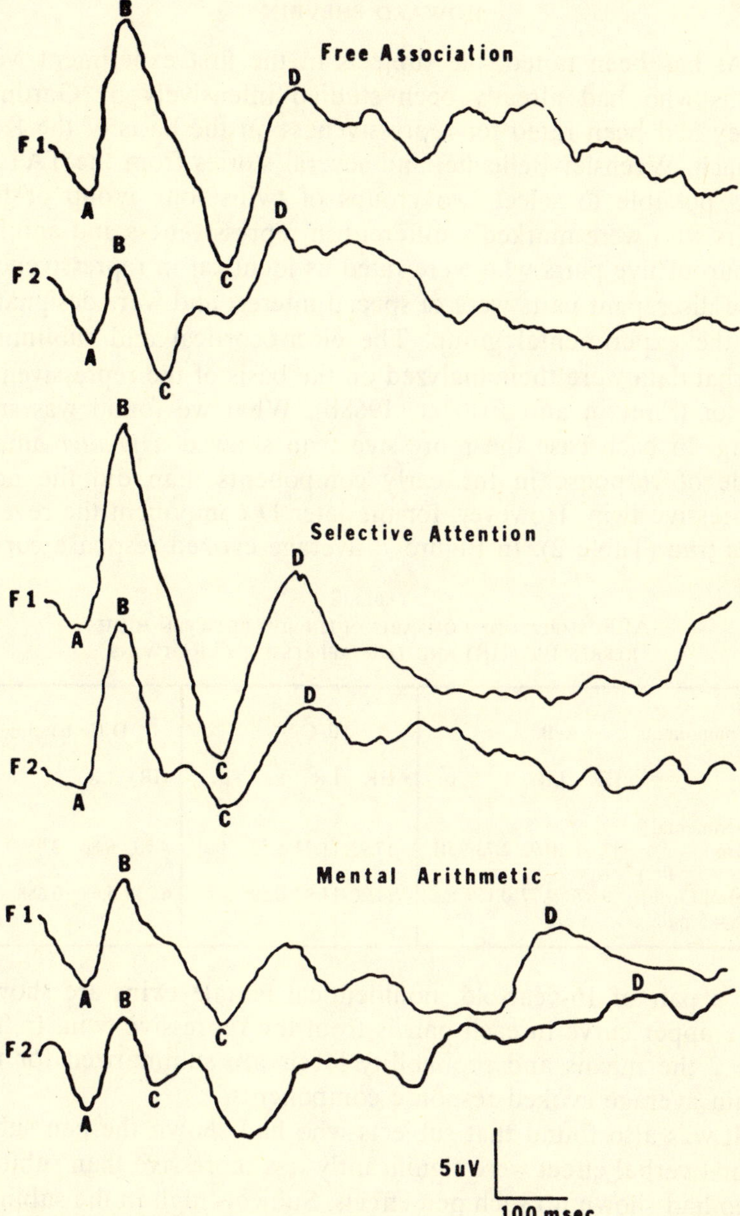

FIGURE 7. AERs for two nonidentical female twins, aged 16 years, 10 months. Upper curve in each pair is from the more repressive twin who was rated 8 for repressiveness as compared to her sister's rating of 5 (both ratings on an 0–10 scale). Components A-B and B-C are appreciably greater for the more repressive twin. Component D, which for the group as a whole is smaller in the more repressive twin, is not as clearly different in this particular pair. The differences between twins in amplitude for the early waves are approximately the same regardless of conditions; this is reflected in the absence of significant interactions of repressiveness and group with conditions.

As has been noted, the subjects in the first experiment were twins who had already been studied intensively by Gardner. They had been rated for repressiveness on the basis of the Rorschach, Wechsler-Bellevue, and several stories from the TAT. It was possible to select two groups of twins: one group of five pairs who were markedly different in repressiveness and another group of five pairs who were rated as identical in repressiveness. The discrepant pairs were of special interest and were designated as the experimental group. The electrocortical and subliminal verbal data were then analyzed on the basis of the repressiveness factor (Shevrin and Fritzler, 1968b). What we found was startling. In each case the repressive twin showed a *greater* amplitude of response in the early components than did the nonrepressive twin. However, for the later D component the reverse was true (Table 2). In Figure 7, average evoked response curves

TABLE 2
AER AMPLITUDE COMPARISON (IN μV) BETWEEN HIGH REPRESSIVE (HR) AND LOW REPRESSIVE (LR) TWINS

AER Components	A–B				B–C				D (to baseline)			
	HR	LR	t	p	HR	LR	t	p	HR	LR	t	p
Experimental Group (N=5 pairs)	12.64	10.92	2.73	.01	17.93	11.74	5.52	.001	4.50	6.86	2.95	.01
Control Group (N=5 pairs)	9.87	9.77	0.159	n.s.	11.20	11.87	0.598	n.s.	6.23	5.68	0.688	n.s.

for a pair of 16-year-old, nonidentical female twins are shown. The upper curve in each pair is from the repressive twin. In Table 2 the means and probability levels are summarized for the main average evoked response components.

It was also found that subjects who had shown the pen subliminal verbal effect were significantly less repressive than subjects who had shown no such pen effects. Subjects high in the subliminal verbal effect showed a diminished evoked response to the external tactile stimulus and were rated as relatively unrepressive. Or, we could say that these subjects could with relative ease shift attention from outside to inside. The repressive personality, on the other hand, finds this shift harder. In fact, we assume that he shifts attention in the opposite direction—from inside to outside for dynamic purposes. This makes good clinical sense, and the combined evoked response and subliminal findings provide reasonably objective support for this clinical view.

However, the increase in some evoked response components and a decrease in a later component seemed at the very least puzzling. In our earlier study we suggested that the D component may be associated with brain processes underlying the verbal responses involved in judging a time interval between successive stimuli and thus may be closely related to judgment and discrimination, whereas the earlier waves might be more closely related to attention. The *decrease* in the D wave for the more repressive subjects may thus be a function of diminished ideational activity. The repressive person intensifies his attention to the stimulus at the expense of thinking about it. One consequence of this inverse relationship may be the concreteness of thinking usually associated with repressiveness. The repressive person may be "caught up" in the perceptual reality of the stimulus while ignoring its connotative implications. He is likely to miss the forest for seeing the trees.

In the Shevrin and Rennick (1967) study we were dealing with a neutral supraliminal stimulus. Subjects were aware of the tap to the index finger and it was by no means a highly charged or meaningful stimulus. What would happen if the stimulus were subliminal and meaningful?

The answer to this question could be obtained by correlating repressiveness ratings with electrocortical amplitudes and free-association verbal effects in the two subliminal studies previously described. In the first subliminal study (Shevrin, Smith, and Fritzler, 1969) repressiveness correlated *negatively* with the early amplitude associated with attention which had discriminated between the subliminal rebus and matched control stimulus. However, the correlations were equally negative for both the meaningful and neutral stimulus. At the supraliminal speed (30 msec.) the correlations became positive, although smaller: the correlation between repressiveness and the average evoked response amplitude for the rebus at the subliminal speed was –.59 ($p < .10$), and at the supraliminal speed it was .49 (*ns*). For the control stimulus the same correlations were –.62 ($p < .10$) and .31

(*ns*). Again we found that in this study R and D acted alike, as if some general factor were at work. All correlations between repressiveness ratings and the subliminal verbal effects were negative. For the first 1 msec. condition the rank-order correlation between knee associates and repression was –.90 ($p < .01$).

In the third experiment (Shevrin, Smith, and Fritzler, 1970), in which the same twin design was used as in the Shevrin and Rennick (1967) experiment, a negative relationship was found between repressiveness and the amplitude for the rebus stimulus only. The nonrepressive twin had a significantly greater response to R than to D as compared to the repressive twin in each pair ($t = 2.453$, df 15, $p < .05$, one-tailed test). Thus, the finding for the meaningful stimulus was replicated. Negative relationships between repressiveness and verbal effects were also present. For the first 1 msec. condition, nonrepressive subjects had more penny associates than repressive subjects (Wilcoxon Signed Rank Test, $p = .05$), and more pen clangs (Wilcoxon Signed Rank Test, $p = .05$). The rebus effect (penny associates) was significantly weaker in the repressive twins than in the nonrepressive twins. Although the relationship between repressiveness and amplitude became positive at 30 msec., it was weaker than in the other two studies. We were unable to obtain a clear replication of this finding at supraliminal speeds.

The pattern of findings with respect to repressiveness is an interesting one: within a fraction of a second (by 260 msec.) the cortical evoked response is already influenced by a repressive factor which is associated with a reduction in the amplitude of a component related to attention. Moreover, the evoked response to a meaningful subliminal stimulus is more definitely influenced than the evoked response to a neutral stimulus. There is a tendency for repressiveness to be associated with an increase in amplitude for supraliminal stimuli. Finally, repressiveness is negatively related to subliminal verbal effects.

Although the evidence is not conclusive, this pattern of findings strongly suggests that specific acts of repression are involved. It is still conceivable that some other general factor, like a diminished responsiveness to stimuli, accounts for these findings. An explanation of this type would encounter difficulty in dealing with the findings from the first study in which an *in-*

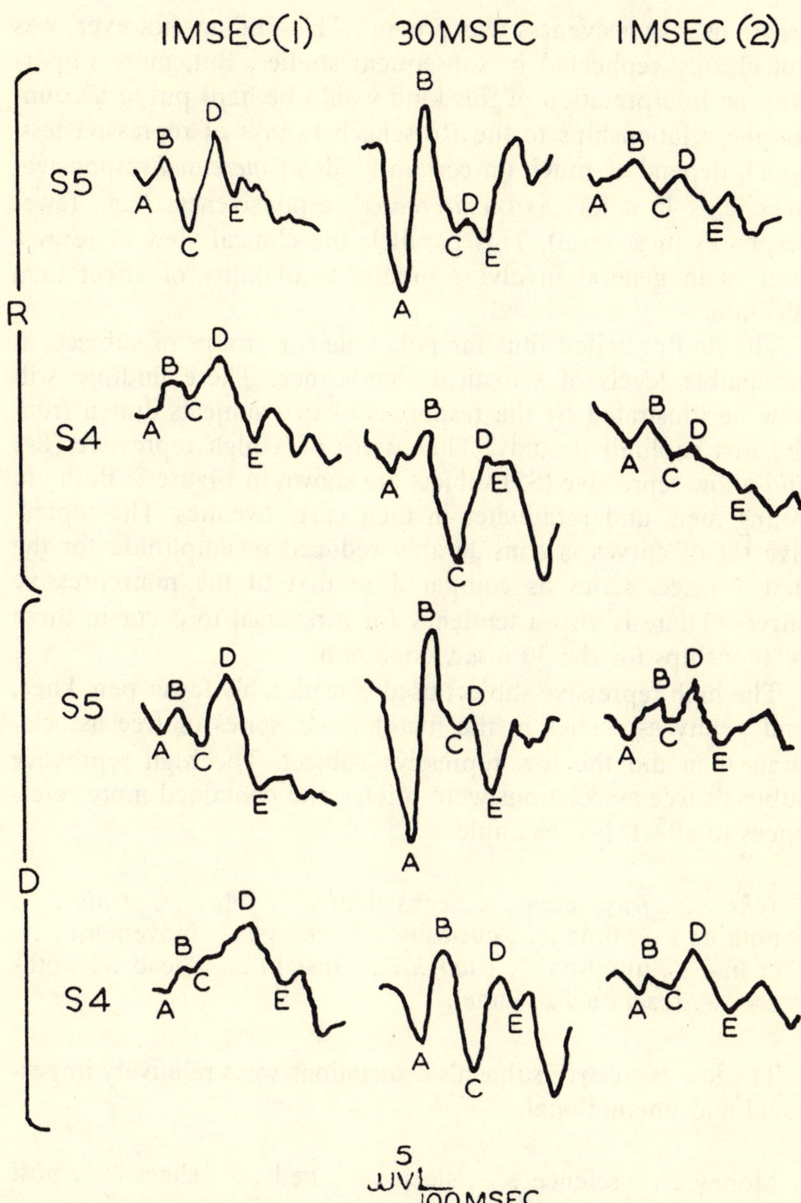

FIGURE 8. Subject 4 is a high repressive subject and Subject 5 is a low repressive subject. The BC component is lower for the PEN/KNEE rebus (R) for Subject 4 than it is for Subject 5 in the first 1 msec. series. The same BC component for the 30 msec. series is slightly larger for the high repressive as compared to the low repressive subject. For the stimulus D the BC component for Subject 4 is absent; the designations assigned on the curve are arbitrary, although they follow certain rules which are applied to all of the curves. Note that the effects diminish in the second 1 msec. series.

crease in responsiveness was present. This finding, however, was not cleanly replicated in subsequent studies. But, more important, an interpretation of this kind would be hard put to account for the relationships to the Rorschach ratings of repressiveness, which depend as much on certain kinds of *increased* responsiveness (e.g., to color) as on *decreased* responsiveness (e.g., fewer responses in general). This parallels the clinical view of repression as in general involving greater availability of affect than ideation.

The findings cited thus far hold true for groups of subjects at acceptable levels of statistical significance. These findings will now be illustrated by the responses of two subjects drawn from the first subliminal study. The curves of a high repressive (S4) and a low repressive (S5) subject are shown in Figure 8. Both are young men, undergraduates in their early twenties. The repressive set of curves is considerably reduced in amplitude for the first 1 msec. series as compared to that of the nonrepressive curves. There is also a tendency for a reversal to occur in these relationships for the 30 msec. condition.

The high repressive subject used considerably fewer pen, knee, and penny associates in the first 1 msec. series of free associations than did the low repressive subject. The high repressive subject's free associations were briefer and contained more references to affect. For example:

> *Joke* . . . *frustration* . . . consistent . . . job . . . *strain* . . . nothing . . . time . . . curiosity . . . *crazy* . . . movement . . . chair . . . question . . . *laugh* . . . insight . . . head . . . others . . . reaction . . . panel.

The low repressive subject's associations were relatively impersonal and unemotional:

> Money . . . science . . . sleep . . . bed . . . sheet . . . post . . . springs . . . radio . . . cigarette . . . Pepsi . . . glass . . . ice . . . magazine . . . hello . . . sweat shirt . . . pajamas . . . loafers . . . socks . . . picture . . . frame . . . cloth . . . metal . . . beer . . . can . . . pitcher . . . glass . . . cardboard . . .

Their Rorschachs were strikingly different. The high repressive subject gave half as many responses as the low repressive subject, yet he gave twice as many responses involving color. His performance was marked by much ready affect and a relative constriction of ideation. To Card II, which contains prominent red areas, he responded with laughter, saying, "Oh, I wish you didn't have to make everything so difficult in the morning!" His two responses to the card were: (1) "Two dancing bears" (said loudly and followed by laughter); (2) "A spaceship."

The low repressive subject was unemotional in his responses to the cards. He gave six responses to Card II: (1) "Two monks kneeling, pressing their hands together," (2) "The red part down here could be a butterfly," (3) "or someone's throat," (4) "and it could represent a jet plane being blown up from the rear with a heat-seeking rocket," (5) "and it might represent a Cheshire cat"; (6) "It might also be some sort of demon or devil–some fantastic creature–strange-looking."

A clinician might be tempted to consider the low repressive subject an obsessive-compulsive personality relying on such defenses as intellectualization, isolation, and reaction formation.

DISCUSSION

The combined subliminal and evoked response methods used in the experiments described in this paper may make it possible to investigate a number of issues heretofore not readily amenable to laboratory study: (1) primary- and secondary-process thinking; (2) the relationship between attention and defenses; (3) psychodiagnosis; (4) psychotherapy research.

1. PRIMARY- AND SECONDARY-PROCESS THINKING

The potential usefulness of the method is nowhere better illustrated than in the findings showing that primary- and secondary-process thinking are associated with different AER parameters. The capacity to discriminate between these two levels of thought organization opens up exciting prospects for studying the psychopathology of thinking. This prospect is especially inviting because the method does not depend on complex levels of clinical inference or intuition (as do therapy records or psychological tests), while staying close to the nature of the phenomena themselves. Apparently, the same subliminal input may be "processed" in a rational, veridical way and in an irrational, unrealistic way. High amplitude of evoked response in a component occurring within the first 260 msec. poststimulus is associated with conceptual-level effects, whereas bursts of alpha occurring at 1.5 sec. poststimulus are associated with clang and rebus effects. Shevrin and Fisher (1967), in their study of the relationship between subliminal stimulation and the sleep-dream cycle referred to earlier, also reported findings which require the assumption that the same subliminal input can be processed on different levels of thought organization which then become conscious in either REM or NREM sleep. If we put the findings from this sleep-dream study together with the findings described in this paper, we can hypothesize that shortly after the subliminal stimulus is flashed the stimulus content is processed and stored in two memory banks, one organized on the basis of secondary-process thinking and the other on the basis of primary-process thinking. Subsequently, when the sleeper enters into stage 1 REM sleep, the "primary-process" memory bank is mainly drawn upon, whereas during stage 2 NREM sleep the "secondary-process" memory bank is mainly drawn upon. The two conditions of thought are apparently separated into different systems of information processing, although in most naturally occurring behavior the two forms are intermingled. For example, in the free associations collected in the experiments, conceptual, clang, and rebus-related words occur in the same stream of thought. The subject might explain (we might say, rationalize) these associations, having such different origins in thought, on some reasonable basis; yet before their appearance in the stream of associations they have been processed in different ways.

2. ATTENTION AND DEFENSES

This topic is much too complex to examine fully in this context. Comments will be limited to the role of attention with respect to repressive defenses. First, the evidence presented makes sense if it is assumed that attention is not limited to consciousness. In the "sense-organ" conception of consciousness, attention is controlled by this superordinate structure: when attention is withheld, a content is presumably kept out of consciousness; when attention is invested in a content, it attains consciousness. But once it is assumed that attention itself can be in the service of *non*conscious structures, the "sense-organ" conceptualization must be radically transformed. For example, when attention is in the service of conscious structures, as in the study involving a supraliminal tactile stimulus, repression is supported by an *intensification* of attention to an external stimulus and a *diminution* of thinking about the stimulus. When attention is in the service of unconscious structures, repression is supported by a *diminution* of attention associated with an *inhibition* of ideation related to the subliminal stimulus. The repressive personality does not uniformly withhold attention in the service of repression. But attention is withheld or invested depending on whether the repressive aim can best be served by *intensification* or *diminution* of attention (H. Schlesinger, 1964). This distinction could perhaps be expressed by referring to the intensification of attention with respect to supraliminal neutral stimuli as *avoidance*, and reserving the term *repression* for the diminution of attention to subliminal inputs. Although the subject may be aware of intensifying his attention to the supraliminal tactile stimulus, one important reason for doing so–to avoid anxiety-arousing ideas–remains unconscious. With respect to subliminal inputs, the entire process is unconscious. According to this view, attention is available to unconscious ego structures, and drive-organized motivational structures can directly mobilize unconscious attention for purposes of subliminal perception. Moreover, at the very start of this subliminal perceptual process, defensive factors may already be at work. Within a fraction of a second a repressive damper is placed on the developing attentional and perceptual processes. Thereafter the consequences in thought are further controlled by repressive or ideational defenses. All of this can take place with awesome rapidity, although the final outcome in some overt response may be considerably delayed. Fisher (1956) suggested this possibility early in the work on subliminal perception.

From an empirical standpoint, one significant weakness of this formulation is that the method does not permit the independent assessment of *unconscious motives.* We do have an independent assessment of subliminal attention, perception, ideation, and repressiveness, but we do not have any idea about the prevailing motives at work which necessitate avoidance and repression. We can, of course, speculate that they must be related to the sexual and/or aggressive implications of the stimulus, but this approach does not provide an *independent* assessment of unconscious motives. We can fall back on the tests, but there too it is not always easy to distinguish between the defense and what specifically is being defended against. We are in need of a methodological innovation which would most likely involve the manipulation of drive states—a hazardous undertaking.

3. PSYCHODIAGNOSIS

We are always in search of refinements in diagnosis, especially those that offer either more efficient or more unambiguous alternatives to what we have. It is not proposed that the method described here is ready for diagnostic application. The Rorschach, the other psychological diagnostic tests, and a good clinical examination are still our best means. But it is conceivable that, with further work and increased understanding, the evoked response method linked with subliminal stimulation will provide a useful adjunct to diagnosis, especially with respect to such part processes as attention, perception, and their interactions with personality factors.

4. PSYCHOTHERAPY RESEARCH

Related to diagnostic issues is the assessment of change as a result of treatment. In the absence of reasonably reliable and objective indications of change, it is difficult to convince the scientific community of the value of expressive psychotherapy and psychoanalysis. It is, of course, necessary to rely on the best methods we currently have, which are mainly clinical evaluations, psychological tests, and ratings of various kinds. At some point in the future, however, it may be possible to assess shifts in defensive organization from a more to a less repressive orientation by evoked response and subliminal stimulation methods.

The advantage of these methods would be in providing a means for assessing defensive shifts entirely independent of clinical evaluation and judgment. This development still lies some distance in the future, but perhaps the distance is less than we have heretofore imagined.

4

SOME DIFFICULTIES IN THE WAY OF PSYCHOANALYTIC RESEARCH: A SURVEY AND A CRITIQUE

PHILIP S. HOLZMAN

Almost three quarters of a century after the first major psychoanalytic publication we have set ourselves the task of seriously discussing scientific tests of many of Freud's assertions. This symposium is in large measure a tribute to the extraordinary scope and brilliance of Freud's ideas. There is no denying that psychoanalytic ideas have dramatically excited literature, the theater, sociology, and psychology itself, as well as the practice of psychiatry and the healing of troubled lives. Whatever one may think of the worth of these ideas, they certainly have stirred things up. But their yield in solid psychological research has been disappointing from the point of view of both the committed psychoanalyst and the research psychologist. Why? I believe that there are at least four reasons for this disappointing yield of psychoanalytic research: (1) the nature of psychoanalytic theory, (2) the inadequate clinical training of research investigators, (3) the poor scientific training offered in psychoanalytic institutes, and (4) the narrow conception of the research task.

1. The nature of psychoanalytic theory. The first barrier to effective research on psychoanalytic ideas lies in the nature of what has been referred to as psychoanalytic theory. What has been called psychoanalytic theory is actually many theories that are loosely tied together—microtheories both psychological and clinical linked with one another. For example, there are psychoanalytic theories of memory, of perception, of attention, of consciousness, of action, of emotion, of concept formation, of development, etc. There is also a complex of clinical theories concerned with psychopathology and with treatment. Some of the "theories" are rather inchoate, are poorly stated, and are in what may be called a pretheoretical form. Some are working models rather than well-constructed theories. Some are extremely far removed from clinical data, and others are generalizations from unique clinical observations. Most of the theories appear in various of Freud's papers. In his monumental but obscure Chapter 7 of *The Interpretation of Dreams* (1900), Freud tried to describe what the psychic apparatus must be like for dreams to occur. In the course of that effort he had to propose a theory of cognition and of consciousness. Eleven years later, in "Formulations on the Two Principles of Mental Functioning" (1911), and again in 1915–1917 when he wrote the "Papers on Metapsychology," he modified the ideas first expressed in *The Interpretation of Dreams*. To read his theories can be confusing, for he never bothered to rework his older formulations in the light of his new conceptions. To take one example, in 1900 Freud discussed consciousness as a sense organ, that is, as an apparatus for receiving but not storing percepts and ideational qualities; but in 1926 he spoke of consciousness as a quality of ideas. Thus, when someone refers to the psychoanalytic conception of consciousness or of attention or of perception, it is hard to know what aspect of psychoanalytic theory, and at what particular time, is being referred to.

Freud never undertook a complete systematization of his theories. Probably his most massive effort at systematizing was Chapter 7 of *The Interpretation of Dreams*. But that was an incomplete job. The theory contained within it was, after all, tied to dreams, and he expressed the conviction that he must tie it as tightly to the phenomena of neurotic behavior for it to be of general psychological value. Despite this conviction, he never completed that task. Indeed, in several papers he mentioned that he felt such an attempt at systematizing was premature, that there were not enough data for him to set down a clinical theory in its final form. In one of his papers he wrote:

> Psycho-analysis is not, like philosophies, a system starting out from a few sharply defined basic concepts, seeking to grasp the whole universe with the help of these and, once it is completed, having no room for fresh discoveries or better understanding. On the contrary, it keeps close to the facts in its field of study, seeks to solve the immediate problems of observation, gropes its way forward by the help of experience, is always incomplete and always ready to correct or modify its theories. There is no incongruity (any more than in the case of physics or chemistry) if its most general concepts lack clarity and if its postulates are provisional; it leaves their more precise definition for the results of future work [1923b, pp. 253–254].

He was clearly quite aware of the looseness of the theoretical structure of psychoanalysis.

2. The inadequate clinical training of research investigators. The second barrier between the rich source of hypotheses and an effective research tradition is the fact that sophisticated research investigators, for the most part, have a poor knowledge of psychoanalysis; and conversely, most psychoanalysts are not skilled methodologists. It would be unthinkable, as Ruth Tolman pointed out, for someone to study the behavior of high-speed particles without a thorough grounding in subatomic physics. Yet many of us do expect psychologists to make research translations of psychoanalytic theories or assertions without an adequate acquaintance with the source materials for these hypotheses—the writings of Sigmund Freud, later elaborations and additions to Freud's hypotheses, and also the clinical situations that gave rise to many of the observations. Few have read completely and in a scholarly manner *The Interpretation of Dreams* (1900), the "Project for a Scientific Psychology" (1895), the two papers on the defense neuropsychoses (1894, 1896), "Formulations on the Two Principles of Mental Functioning" (1911), "On Narcissism" (1914), "Instincts and Their Vicissitudes" (1915a), "The Unconscious" (1915b), "Repression" (1915c), "Negation" (1925a), "A Note upon the 'Mystic Writing-Pad'" (1925b), and some have not even read the better-known works, "Beyond the Pleasure Principle" (1920), "The Ego and the Id" (1923a), and "Inhibitions, Symptoms and Anxiety" (1926). I venture to say that there are few psychologists versed in the techniques of research who have read and understood these works. Yet psychoanalysis is part of psychology, a source of rich insights into human behavior, and it should not be left by default to those who tend to make it only a method of treatment and, at that, one suited for only a limited number of people.

3. The poor scientific training offered in psychoanalytic institutes. A third reason for the poor yield of psychoanalytic reasearch is related to the organization of psychoanalytic institutes and societies. It seems that "organized psychoanalysis"—which is not to be identified with the body of psychoanalytic knowledge—has had a policy of accepting only psychiatrists for training in clinical psychoanalysis. Such a policy has had the effect of making psychoanalysis more of a service and the training centers more like trade schools. But it has also barred talented nonmedical researchers from the wellspring of psychoanalytic observations—the clinical psychoanalytic situation. It is therefore rather refreshing to see that in a few quarters this situation is slowly being corrected.

4. The narrow conception of the research task. A fourth impediment to psychoanalytic research is the limits which many investigators place on the scientific endeavor in general, and on the investigation of psychoanalytic hypotheses in particular. The studies discussed by Sears (1943) and many subsequent studies (with a few noteworthy exceptions) up to the present time suggest that the investigators conceived of psychoanalytic research in terms of taking a psychoanalytic idea or statement and attempting to confirm or disprove it. Such an approach is generally unproductive. It is a waste of talent for a skilled investigator to spend his life disproving and debunking theories which he found useless in the first place, or confirming those in which he believed all along. The fruitfulness of psychoanalytic ideas, in general, is their potential for generating new hypotheses about behavior and for pointing in directions to look for novel discoveries, hitherto unknown relationships, and unsuspected sources of variance.

THE NATURE OF PSYCHOANALYTIC RESEARCH

What is the nature of the psychoanalytic approach? Psychoanalysis developed as an empirical but not as an experimental science. It developed from clinical data. Freud's subjects were patients who came to him displaying bizarre hysterical symptoms such as contractures, paralyses, and tics, and he felt compelled to try to explain these strange symptoms. Before Freud's attempts to explain neurotic symptoms in 1894 and 1896, psychiatrists looked upon hysterical symptoms as the results of "degenerate constitutions," accident, or somatic disposition. Freud's great contribution in that last decade of the nineteenth century was the formulation of two assumptions: (1) that hysterical symptoms are primarily mental phenomena, psychological although not necessarily conscious; and (2) that they have a meaning, that is, they can be understood, they can be explained, and they are psychologically determined. Indeed, these two postulates, psychologism and determinism, are probably the only two aspects of Freud's theory that have remained intact from 1894 to the present. All other aspects Freud or others modified in one way or another. The modifications, moreover, were spurred by constantly increasing clinical experience. Freud always insisted that psychoanalytic theory must change in the wake of new findings. Here is one example of how clinical experience and thinking about his subject matter forced him to change his theory.

In 1894, Janet, Breuer, and Charcot had explained hysterical symptoms by the assumption that a "splitting of consciousness" had occurred which permitted these strange symptoms to exist alongside of more or less normal behavior and thinking. But they did not explain with any consistency or cogency the etiology of the splitting. Janet assumed that splitting occurred on the basis of an innate constitutional weakness. Breuer assumed that it occurred on the basis of hypnoid states. In both explanations, a theory of motivation was lacking. It was this theory that Freud supplied. Freud's explanation did not emphasize heredity, for Freud learned from most of his patients that they had enjoyed good health up until the time of the illness. His patients, however, told him of experiences–usually sexual in nature–that were so distressing that they had tried to forget about them because they could not resolve the incompatibility between these distressing experiences or ideas and their own moral character. He did not think that this desire to forget was in any way pathological, for he noted that, indeed, many people who had had similar experiences successfully forgot the incompatible ideas and remained healthy. But Freud's patients were not successful in forgetting. It was this failure to forget that he regarded as disposing the patient to pathological states. Freud saw no need here to assume any hereditary degeneracy.

Freud reasoned that since the patient could not eradicate the memory of the distressing event the idea of it persisted, accompanied by the painful affect associated with it. He assumed that the intense affect was the main source of the distress and that the patient could somehow decrease the distress by weakening the affect by some means. He assumed that in hysteria this was accomplished by converting the affect into some kind of somatic innervation. The particular organs so innervated were symbolically and cognitively connected or associated with the distressing experience. The problem for the patient then became only the memory as represented by the motor or sensory innervation. This formulation required Freud to assume that affects could be transformed. He stated this assumption in quantitative language:

> I should like, finally, to dwell for a moment on the working hypothesis which I have made use of in this exposition. . . . I refer to the concept that in mental functions something is to be distinguished—a quota of affect or sum of excitation—which possesses all the characteristics of a quantity (though we have no means of measuring it), which is capable of increase, diminution, displacement and discharge, and which is spread over the memory-traces of ideas somewhat as an electric charge is spread over the surface of a body [1894, p. 60].

Two years later, in 1896, he considered his theory of hysteria quite incomplete. He wondered why it was that some patients were able to have experiences that were incompatible with their moral standards *without* ever developing hysteria. He needed to hypothesize a predisposition to hysteria. Again, this predisposition was conceived of not as hereditary but as the result of an earlier experience. He did not invent this predisposition solely because his theory needed an explanation of why trauma in later life precipitated hysteria. It is true that he needed to explain the issue of individual differences—i.e., why some persons and not others develop hysteria. But his *patients* kept referring to earlier events in their childhood and invariably, in 20 out of 20 cases he reported, they referred to early sexual seductions, that is, to passive sexual experiences. Freud then assumed that the experiences after puberty which precipitate a hysterical attack do so because they arouse the memory of the first sexual attack, releasing the affect of the early trauma and triggering motivated forgetting.

The first primitive theory of psychopathology underwent many changes. In the first theory, Freud assumed only that for neurosis to occur there must be a conflict between the memory of a real event and one's moral standards. There was no mention of drives, of impulses, or of psychosexual development. That came later. Even a systematic conception of unconscious mental processes was not there, although it was implicit in the theory that mental events can take place out of awareness and indeed that those events have noteworthy effects on behavior.

The rest of the story is rather well-known. Freud soon discovered that he had been taken in by his patients' "memories." The childhood seductions that they described were not real events but fantasies. On the basis of this discovery, Freud felt he had to explain the apparent universality of these fantasies in his patients. He now concluded that these wishes, daydreams, or fantasies were based on the patients' own sexual activity during childhood. Freud later developed his epigenetic theory of psychosexual development. Although the special theory of psychosexual development is probably the most popularized part of the body of psychoanalytic assertions, it is by no means the foundation of psychoanalysis. The cornerstones of psychoanalytic theory remain (1) that behavior can be thought of in psychological terms and can be explained by lawful relations; (2) that much that is mental can exist outside the realm of consciousness and indeed does exist outside the realm of consciousness and influences consciousness and behavior; and (3) that behavior is fundamentally, although not exclusively, directed by drives.

Now, if one grants the contention that psychoanalytic ideas developed from observational data, that the theory is inductive, then one can give it a dignified place as an empirical science alongside experimental science. A pressing question is one of timing, that is, when it is appropriate for ultimate experimental validation of psychoanalytic formulations to occur. My emphasis in answering this question is different from that demanded by a strict operationalist or positivist approach. One must guard against nipping preliminary exploration in the bud; there needs to be a period in which curiosity and inquiry into the unique and novel should not be formalized but should wait for some results of natural observation, for we can experiment only on what we have already observed and comprehended. As Martin Scheerer (1945–1946) said, explanations of phenomena and their reduction to scientific laws can only follow, and not precede, the observation of the phenomenon we seek to understand. Robert Oppenheimer (1956, p. 135) wrote: "It is not always tactful to try to quantify; it is not always clear that by measuring one has found something very much worth measuring. . . . It is a real property of the real world that you are measuring, but it is not necessarily the best way to advance true understanding of what is going on . . ." I believe that a premature rigor in some psychoanalytic research is one of the reasons for the inadequacy of such research. Yet the opposite difficulty also obtains, and a casual indifference to controls, to quantities, to instruments of observation, to replicability has characterized much poor work that masquerades as psychoanalytic research.

Let me describe briefly what I believe is the nature of psychoanalytic research. There are at least four areas in which research germane to psychoanalysis can be done.

1. The first area is the study of psychoanalytic technique itself. Does it have therapeutic efficacy? What goes on in the therapeutic relationship?

2. One can use the psychoanalytic method itself to confirm hypotheses about behavior, or to formulate and discover certain lawful relationships, particularly about intrapsychic experiences. This is the method adopted by Lester Luborsky.

3. Some experimenters have no explicit psychoanalytic intent, yet their experiments and their results are relevant to psychoanalytic theory. I have in mind here, for example, the studies of sensory isolation, the work of Bartlett on memory, of Werner and Wapner and their colleagues on thinking, of Piaget on the development of intelligence.

4. Finally, one may choose to investigate some aspects of the theory itself. For example, one may investigate consciousness, or registration, or the problem of how it is that we perceive so accu-

rately in spite of the influence of motives on our perceptions. The work of George S. Klein and his colleagues, of Donald Spence, and of Howard Shevrin are examples of this approach.

In my opinion, then, psychoanalysis is a rich body of hypotheses, and if one seeks to check these ideas by any valid investigatory method he is doing psychoanalytic research. The dedicated psychological investigator should have no vested interest in whether aspects of psychoanalytic theory are confirmed or refuted. It would not shatter the foundations of psychoanalysis, for example, if one were to discover that psychosexual development takes place in a manner different from the way analysts now assume it develops.

Let us turn to the specifics of the three examples of psychoanalytic research presented in this volume. All three research examples address themselves to the question of the fate of ideas that are out of the reach of awareness. Actually, the experimental investigation of such phenomena began before the development of psychoanalysis. Helmholtz, Binet, Urbantschitsch, and Johannes Müller showed much interest in studying noticed and unnoticed visual phenomena. Even in Titchener's laboratory, studies of weak percepts and their effects on images proceeded quite independent of psychoanalytic developments (e.g., Perky, 1910). It was, of course, Pötzl's experiments in 1917 that sparked the interest of psychoanalysts in these effects. Psychoanalysts took interest in this area of investigation principally because of Freud's theory of the process of dreaming. In *The Interpretation of Dreams* (1900), Freud proposed that experiences of the day find their way into the dream only if they have never been conscious or have had consciousness withdrawn from them. He distinguished five classes of such day residues: (1) tasks left incomplete because of an interruption, (2) tasks left incomplete because of an inability or failure, (3) suppressed acts or thoughts, (4) unconscious thoughts which have been stimulated by preconscious thoughts, and (5) indifferent incidental impressions. These various kinds of experiences have an activating and recruiting effect precisely because they are without the scrutiny of attention. But, curiously, only the Allers and Teler experiment in 1924 intervened between Pötzl's work and the experimental series by Fisher (1956). The history of these experiments and their criticisms and countercriticisms are well presented by Fisher (1960), Pine (1964), Eriksen (1960), and Goldiamond (1958, 1962). From these studies some solid findings have emerged: stimuli become percepts—that is, consciously discriminated and therefore noticed—only in the context of awareness. Stimuli that do not reach awareness—because they are either too weak, too fleeting, or too incidental—are, however, not without effect, for there is sufficient evidence that such stimuli do exert an influence on imagery, thought content, and subsequent discrimination. Although such effects are slight, they are nonetheless measurable.

In this volume Spence clarifies much of the early work on marginal stimuli by exploring some of the conditions such stimulation must meet in order to exert specific effects on thought. Shevrin probes whether registrations without awareness undergo singularly different organizational fates than do those stimuli which are accompanied by conscious discrimination. Luborsky focuses on the psychoanalytic situation itself and investigates naturally occurring fleeting ideas.

Luborsky's paper breaks new ground. It exploits the psychoanalytic situation for experimental and research purposes in a way not attempted before. The empirical data gathered by Freud occurred in a unique setting, one in which a patient who has been experiencing personal suffering agrees to say to the analyst whatever comes to his mind. He further agrees not to censor anything and, by dint of his suffering and by the therapeutic intent of the analyst, he is presumed to be highly motivated to stick to that rule. Such a situation indeed occurs in no other psychological laboratory. But how strange that no one really has been able to exploit this situation in a productive way beyond Freud's therapeutic use of it. Yet since this situation is the source of psychoanalytic data and of psychoanalytic hypotheses, it is unfortunate that its research development has been lacking.

More ingenuity is required for the research use of the free-association method than the analyst's abandoning himself to his own observations and impressions. Luborsky's study is the first I know of to make research use of this situation. He uses it imaginatively and with unquestioned originality. He takes a phenomenon which can best be closely observed in the psychoanalytic situation—momentary forgetting—and scrutinizes it.

He describes it, notes its frequency, its context, its temporal characteristics, etc. He works like a biologist, specifying the structure of what it is he sees and then trying to classify it with other phenomena. Thus far the research technique that Luborsky has adopted is a nonexperimental one. He then invokes the psychoanalytic bias of looking for the significance, meaning, and purpose of the phenomenon. He assumes that momentary forgetting serves a purpose and that it occurs for a very personal reason. Luborsky asks if there is any regularity in its occurrence. At this point he begins to work as an experimenter, creating control groups and control protocols and asking judges to match records and make inferences about the protocols. This may be the weakest and strongest point of the study. For when one looks for purposes underlying the momentary forgetting, one is forced to compare those purposes with those of other phenomena or momentary symptoms, such as coughing or the urge to urinate. That is, one is obliged to ask how specific the purpose is. Yet the unique bias of psychoanalysis consists in specifying that these microsymptoms serve purposes.

Luborsky's work is incomplete, but the directions are clear. A kind of successive comparison of purposes would be in order: Does momentary forgetting serve a unique function which is different from, say, the functions served by occasional borborygmus or urinary urgency during psychoanalytic sessions? Luborsky does not ask these questions and therefore he leaves unanswered the question of motivational specificity.[1]

Another significant problem that Luborsky's work points to is the storage and retrieval of psychoanalytic data. The psychoanalytic therapeutic session produces a wealth of verbal material which for the most part is neither stored nor retrieved. It is a source of material waiting for some investigators to ask meaningful questions of it. I am reminded of the anecdote told about Gertrude Stein on her deathbed. As the famous writer lay dying, her friend, Alice B. Toklas, was alleged to have bent near her and asked, "Gertrude, what is the answer? Tell me, what is the answer?" To which Miss Stein is supposed to have replied, "Al-

[1] However, in a study comparing the conditions for momentary forgetting with those for migraine headache and stomach pains, he attempts to deal with the 'ssue of specificity (Luborsky and Auerbach, 1969).

ice, what is the question?" There is a wealth of untapped potential in psychoanalytic interviews, but the problem is to formulate significant questions and then to get answers out of the material. Merely to tape-record the psychoanalytic interview is not, of course, the answer to the problem of retrieval. Tape-recording is surely better than not recording the interview, but the tapes are still only raw data. It would be a Herculean task to try to get data out of 600 tape-recorded hours if one thought of a researchable question only after, not before, the data were recorded. And then the problem of reducing those data to some meaningful form remains. Luborsky is not at all satisfied with his segmenting and counting. He realizes that much of the meaning of momentary forgetting is not yet extracted. Perhaps this is because he has not yet been able to ask the key questions of the data.

Donald Spence has addressed himself not to the psychoanalytic situation but to a fundamental assumption of psychoanalytic theory: that fantasies, and particularly fantasies that are outside of awareness, exert steering effects on ideation and behavior. Spence comes up with the finding that our thoughts are not totally at the mercy of unconscious fantasies. That is, after all, no news to us. But we are faced with the following question: If we are motivated by drives and impulses—whose psychological manifestations are unconscious fantasies—what prevents them from steering our behavior in defiance of reality requirements? Spence's results answer: our personal histories, character structure, and chance priming of the fantasy by some experience—in his experiment a flashed word—all must coalesce to affect conscious ideation in specific predictable ways. The experiment presents cogent evidence against the assumption of a pure tyranny of drives. Spence shows us some of the controls over drive experience and, conversely, some of the conditions under which drive can recruit thought for its expression.

Woven into the fabric of Spence's experiment are the various metapsychological points of view which psychoanalysis requires for an explanation of behavior. These are (1) genetic considerations (the personal history of reinforcement); (2) dynamic considerations (the contemporary conflict, in this instance the conflicts attending rejection); (3) topographic considerations (the issue of awareness); (4) structural considerations (the enduring personal style of expressing conflict); and (5) adaptive considerations (response to the restraints of the experimental situation).

To stop at this point is premature, for cross-validation of this experiment is required for the results to be conclusive, particularly since the experimental demonstration rests upon an interaction of variables. Will priming in another independent group produce the same results? Too often experimenters stop after one demonstration of a significant result. It would be preferable if a single demonstration were followed by several replications. The effects Spence examines are too subtle to be left after only one demonstration, however fascinating and compelling.

Shevrin imports a neurophysiological technique to explore the organization of thought following briefly exposed stimuli. He also concerns himself with the psychoanalytic conception of attention and consciousness. He first asks whether stimulus registrations that occur too fast for conscious apprehension undergo a fate different from those that register with full awareness. Some of the considerations are similar to those of Binet, Urbantschitsch, and the Titchenerian structuralists (e.g., Perky, 1910), but Shevrin's concerns go further. He is concerned with a model of psychological functioning that takes account of internal motivations and the organization of unconscious thinking. It is this latter preoccupation rather than the methods that he employs that gives Shevrin's studies their psychoanalytic cast.

If one keeps in mind the caution *not* to equate measurements of little-understood physical processes, like the electrical activity observed from the surface of the scalp, with psychological events, experiences, and processes like attention, then Shevrin's adaptation of the evoked response technique for these purposes is intriguing. With the method of cortical evoked responses he has discovered that alpha-wave activity occurs during free associations, a finding that opens avenues of inquiry into the unique properties of various states of awareness. Free associations may indeed occur in the context of a state of awareness that is distinctly different from that which occurs when one talks directly to a therapist. The recent work of Kamiya (1964) suggests that one can learn to induce in oneself such states of consciousness.

The first experiment discussed by Shevrin confirms for humans the finding of Hernández-Peón, Scherrer, and Jouvet (1956) that vicissitudes of attention can attenuate stimulus input at some point in the registration process, and that such gating can be objectively monitored in electrocortical responses.

On the issue of whether stimuli registered without awareness undergo a fate different from those that register with awareness, the rebus technique he employs does not produce a clear answer. My preference would be to assume that it is not the fate of the stimuli that is different, inasmuch as we cannot see the fates of the quickly exposed stimuli themselves. Rather it is their *influence* on subsequent registrations or thoughts which differs. Here the evidence is compelling: previous workers have demonstrated that weak stimuli are less restrained by context than are strong stimuli. But so are stimuli that were once conscious but are no longer so. The mere fact that a stimulus is in the spotlight of consciousness seems to limit its influence on those socially validated patterns that have relatively strong mutual coherence. Without consciousness, that coherence of ideas is loosened. It is therefore understandable that stimulus registrations out of awareness are more easily recruited to the expression of drives. It seems that the registration of stimuli exposed too fast for effective conscious apprehension is but a special case of the more general condition of being without the restraining influence of consciousness. Shevrin's novel methods capture some of the hitherto elusive vicissitudes of word, idea, and fantasy restructuring that take place outside of awareness.

Shevrin addresses himself to redefinitions and reformulations of psychoanalytic terms, and to that extent he differs from Luborsky and Spence, who explore the motivational influences on certain behavior. Shevrin concludes that attention can be unconscious as well as conscious. Before one can decide on the adequacy of Shevrin's conclusions, one must know his definitions of attention, consciousness, and perception, since he is proposing the concept of "unconscious attention," a term which differs from Freud's definition of attention as that "hypercathexis" which is necessary for awareness. Perhaps all Shevrin means is that stimuli can *register* with and without attention or consciousness, and if stimuli register without consciousness, they are not on that account without influence on thought or subsequent perception. This conclusion is similar to Klein's, and no radical reshuffling of terms is necessary. But if Shevrin equates *registration* without awareness with the *entire perceptual process* and therefore with a perceptual *discrimination,* he does indeed face an apparent self-contradiction in the term "unconscious processes that are attended to." His formulation would need to include a redefinition of *attention* (which would be broader than the "hypercathexis" that permits preconscious ideas to become conscious). He would also need to confront the body of experimental data supporting the proposition that discrimination—as distinguished from sensory input and registration—occurs only where there is some awareness of cues, although verbal report may be unrevealing (e.g., Eriksen, 1960; Goldiamond, 1958). Otherwise, it seems to me, the unique properties of *consciousness* fade.

A few words about the experimental procedures. The experimenter measures the presence of a rebus, clang, or conceptual associate to the pen and knee stimuli by comparing a subject's association with norms established by a group of college students, rather than with the subject's personal associates to those words. Such a comparison as the one Shevrin used may actually obscure the various effects looked for, and weaken the cogency of his results.

The results of experiments testing the effects of presleep stimuli on dreams are typically small effects which require high-powered statistical tools to discern. Therefore, as with Spence's study, replication is desirable.

Finally, the issue of the effects of repression. As Shevrin points out, his experiment posed to his subjects no obvious threat, and, therefore, no actual motive to repress. Shevrin correctly notes that his measure of repression actually assesses proneness-to-make-use-of-repression-in-certain-circumstances. It therefore seems unparsimonious to assume that an act of repression is responsible for the diminished cortical evoked response obtained in his experiment. One can, however, reasonably conclude either that a repressive style of thought organization is associated with a certain typical amplitude of evoked response, or that both repressive style and the associated evoked response amplitude reflect an as yet unidentified third process.

All in all, the experimental situation and results are intriguing, and the methods—both the rebus technique and the ingenious use of cortical evoked responses—have great potential usefulness.

Psychoanalysis as a point of view of behavior—Waelder stated that it is the point of view of conflict—has been a rich source of hypotheses encompassing microscopic and macroscopic conditions. Imaginative research on these ideas can enrich psychology. What is required is a marriage of sophisticated awareness of psychoanalytic ideas with investigatory skills. My conviction is that the offspring of such a union will bring us further understanding of behavior.

5

SOME METHODOLOGICAL REFLECTIONS ON THE DIFFICULTIES OF PSYCHOANALYTIC RESEARCH

PAUL E. MEEHL

Being here in the somewhat ill-defined role of a "methodologist," I shall first make a few general comments reflecting my own views on philosophy of science. Since it is impossible to develop or defend them in a few pages, let me simply say that these views accord generally with the consensus of those who claim expertise–if such exists, as I believe–in that field. That they are not widely accepted in psychology reflects a failure to keep up with developments, many psychologists still espousing a philosophical position that is some 30 years out of date.

Whatever the verisimilitude (Popper, 1959, 1962) of Freud's theories, it will surely be a matter of comment by future historians of science that a system of ideas which has exerted such a powerful and pervasive influence both upon professional practitioners and contemporary culture should, two thirds of a century after the promulgation of its fundamental concepts, still remain a matter of controversy. That fact in itself should lead us to suspect that there is something methodologically peculiar about the relation of psychoanalytic concepts to their evidential base, and I suppose the very existence of this symposium testifies to that peculiarity.

Let me begin by saying that I reject what has come to be called "operationism" as a logical reconstruction of scientific theories. Practically all empiricist philosophers (e.g., Carnap, Feigl, Feyerabend, Hempel, Popper, Sellars)–thinkers who can-

The author is indebted to the Carnegie Corporation of New York for Support of Research via summer appointments as a staff member of the Minnesota Center for Philosophy of Science.

not by any stretch of the imagination be considered muddle-headed, obscurantist, or antiscientific in their sympathies—have for many years recognized that strict operationism (in anything like the form originally propounded by Bridgman) is philosophically indefensible. (But see Wilson, 1967, 1968). In saying this, they do not, however, prejudge those issues of scientific research *strategy* that arise between a quasi operationist like Skinner and a psychoanalytic theorist. And it is commendable that Skinner and his followers (unlike some psychologists) have been careful to avoid invoking "philosophy of science" in their advocacy of either substantive views or research strategy.

Associated with my rejection of operationism is the recognition that biological and social sciences are forced to make use of what have come to be known (following the late logician Arthur Pap, 1953, 1958; see also Cronbach and Meehl, 1955) as "open concepts," the "openness" of these concepts having two or three distinguishable aspects which space does not permit me to develop here. One important consequence of this openness is that we must reject Freud's monolithic claim that it is necessary to accept or reject psychoanalysis as a whole. This is simply false as a matter of formal logic, even in explicitly formalized and clearly interpreted theoretical systems, and such a systematic "holism" is a fortiori untenable when we are dealing with what is admittedly a loose, incomplete, and unformalized conceptual system like psychoanalysis. It is well-known that proper subsets of postulates in physics, chemistry, astronomy, and genetics are continually being changed without "changing everything else" willy-nilly, and it is absurd to suppose that psychoanalytic theory, unlike these advanced sciences, is a corpus of propositions so tightly interknit that they have to be taken "as a whole."

I would also reject any requirement that there should be a *present mapping* of psychoanalytic concepts against constructs at another level of analysis, such as neurophysiology or learning theory. All that one can legitimately require is that psychoanalytic concepts not be *incompatible* with well-corroborated theories of the learning process or nervous-system function. But the situation in these two fields is itself so controversial that this negative requirement imposes only a very weak limitation upon psychoanalytic theorizing.

I would also combat the tendency (found in some psychonomes) to treat the terms "experimental" and "empirical" as synonymous. An enterprise can be empirical (in the sense of taking publicly observable data as its epistemic base) *without* being experimental (in the sense of laboratory manipulation of the variables). Such respectable sciences as astronomy, geography, ecology, paleontology, and human genetics are obvious examples. We should not conflate different dimensions such as the following: experimental-naturalistic; quantitative-qualitative; objective-subjective; documentary-behavioral. It is obvious, for example, that one can carry out objective and quantitative analysis upon a nonexperimental document (e.g., diary, personal correspondence, jury protocol).

I should make clear that while I am not an "orthodox Popperian," I find myself more in sympathy with the logic and methodology of science expounded by Sir Karl Popper (1959, 1962; and see Bunge, 1964) than with that of any other single contemporary thinker. While I share with my Minnesota colleagues Feigl and Maxwell reservations about Sir Karl's complete rejection of what he calls "inductivism," I agree with Popper in emphasizing the extent to which theoretical concepts (often implicit) pervade even the so-called "observation language" of science and of common life; and I incline to accept refutability (falsifiability) as the best criterion to demarcate science from other kinds of cognitive enterprises such as metaphysics.

There is a certain tension between these views. What I have said about operationism, open concepts, and the scientific status of nonexperimental investigation makes life easier for the psychoanalytic theorist; but the Popperian emphasis upon falsifiability tends in the opposite direction.

As a personal note, I may say that, as is true of most psychologists seriously interested in psychoanalysis, I have found my own experience on the couch, and my clinical experience listening to the free associations of patients, far more persuasive than any published research purporting to test psychoanalytic theory. I do not assert that this is a good or a bad thing; I just want to have it down in the record. In the "context of discovery" (Reichenbach, 1938; but see Lakatos, 1968) this very characteristic attitude is worth keeping in mind.

The inventor of psychoanalysis took the same view, and it might be good research strategy to concentrate attention upon the verbal behavior of the analytic session itself. If there is any strong empirical evidence in support of Freud's ideas, that is perhaps the best place to look, since that is where he hit upon them in the first place. We have today the advantage which he regretted not having, that recording an analysand's verbal behavior is a simple and inexpensive process. Skinner points out that what makes the science of behavior difficult is *not*–contrary to the usual view in psychoanalytic writing–problems of *observation,* because (compared with the phenomena of most other sciences) behavior is relatively macroscopic and slow. The difficult problems arise in slicing the pie, that is, in classifying intervals of the behavior flux and in subjecting them to powerful conceptual analysis and appropriate statistical treatment. Whatever one may think of Popper's view that theory subtly infects even so-called observational statements in physics, it is pretty obviously true in psychology because of the trivial fact that an interval of the behavior flux can be sliced up or categorized in different ways. Even in the animal case the problems of response class and stimulus equivalence arise, although less acutely. A patient in an analytic session says, "I suppose you are thinking that this is really about my father, but you're mistaken, because it's not." We can readily conceive of a variety of rubrics under which this chunk of verbal behavior could be plausibly subsumed. We might classify it syntactically, as a complex compound sentence, or as a negative sentence; or as resistance, since it rejects a possible interpretation; or as negative transference, because it is an attribution of error to the analyst; or, in case the analyst has not been having any such associations as he listens, we can classify it as an instance of projection; or as an instance of "father theme"; or we might classify it as self-referential, because its subject matter is the patient's thoughts rather than the thoughts or actions of some third party; and so on and on. The problem here is not mainly one of "reliability" in categorizing, although goodness knows that is a tough one too. Thorough training to achieve perfect interjudge scoring agreement *per rubric* would still leave us with the problem I am raising.

In methodological discussion there are two opposite mistakes which may be made about the evidential value of verbal output in a psychoanalytic hour. One mistake is to demand that there should be a straightforwardly computable numerical probability attached to each substantive idiographic hypothesis, of the sort which we can usually compute with regard to the option of rejecting a statistical hypothesis. This mistake arises from identifying "rationality in inductive inference" with "statistical hypothesis testing." One need merely make this identification explicit to realize that it is a methodological mistake. It would, for instance, condemn as "nonrational" all assessment of substantive scientific theories, or the process of inference in courts of law, or evaluation of theories in such disciplines as history or paleontology. No logician has succeeded in constructing any such automatic numerical "evidence-quantifying" rules, and many logicians and statisticians doubt whether such a thing could be done, even in principle. It is obvious, for instance, that a jury can be put in possession of a pattern of evidence which makes it highly rational to infer beyond a reasonable doubt that the defendant is guilty; but no one (with the exception of Poisson in a famous ill-fated effort) has tried to *quantify* this evidential support in terms of the probability calculus. Whether a distinction can be made between quantifying the corroboration of nomothetic theories (an algorithm for which, says Lakatos [1968, p. 324], is precluded by Church's theorem) and quantifying the probability of particularistic (= idiographic) hypotheses is difficult to say, although we should pursue that line of thought tenaciously. Ideally, I suggest, a Bayes-rule calculation on the idiographic constructions of psychoanalysis should be possible.

The opposite error is the failure to realize that Freud's "jigsaw-puzzle" analogy does not really fit the psychoanalytic hour, because it is simply not true (as he admits elsewhere) that all of the pieces fit together, or that the criteria of "fitting" are tight enough to make it analogous even to a clear-cut criminal trial. Two points, opposite in emphasis but compatible: Anyone who has experienced analysis, practiced it, or listened to taped sessions, if he is halfway fair-minded, will agree that (1) there are sessions in which the material "fits together" so beautifully that one is sure almost any skeptic would be convinced, and (2) there are sessions in which the "fit" is very loose and underdetermined (fewer equations than unknowns, so to speak), this latter kind of session (unfortunately) predominating.

The number of theoretical variables available, and the fact that the theory itself makes provision for their countervailing one another and reversing qualities (e.g., the dream work's sometime expression of content by opposites), lead to the ever-present possibility that the ingenuity of the human mind will permit the therapist to impose a construction which, while it has a certain *ad hoc* plausibility, nevertheless has low verisimilitude. What we would like to have is a *predictive* criterion, but the trouble is that the theory does not claim to make, in most cases, highly specific content predictions. Thus, as Freud himself pointed out, while we can sometimes make a plausible case for the occurrence of certain latent dream thoughts which were transformed via the dream work into the manifest content of a dream, the same set of dream thoughts *could* have been responsible for a completely different manifest content. Similarly, in paleontology, the fossil data may be rationally taken to support the theory of evolution, but there is nothing in the theory of evolution that enables us to predict that such an organism as the rhinoceros will have been evolved, or that we should find fossil trilobites. Or, again, the facts may strongly support the hypothesis that the accused had a motive and the opportunity, so he murdered the deceased; but these assumptions would be equally compatible with his having murdered him at a different time and place, and by the use of a knife rather than a revolver. I do not myself have any good solution to this difficulty. The best I can come up with is that, lacking a rigorous mathematical model for the dream work, and lacking any adequate way of estimating the strengths of the various initial conditions that constitute parameters in the system, we should at least be able to apply crude counting statistics, such as theme frequencies, to the verbal output during the later portions of the hour when these are predicted (by psychoanalytically skilled persons) from the output at the beginning of the hour. I look in this direction because of my clinical impression that one's ability to forecast the *general theme* of the associative material from the manifest content of the dream plus the initial associations to it, while far from perfect, is nevertheless often good enough to constitute the kind of clinical evidence that carries the heaviest weight with those who open-mindedly but skeptically embark upon psychoanalytic work. Let me give a concrete example (one on which I myself would be willing to lay odds of 90 to 10, and not on a mere "significant difference" but on an almost complete predictability within the limits of the reliability of thematic classification). If a male patient dreams about fire and water, or dreams about one and quickly associates to the other (and here the protocol scoring would be a straightforward, objective, almost purely clerical job approaching perfect interscorer reliability), the dominant theme in the remainder of the session will involve *ambition* as a motive and *shame* (or triumph) as an affect. In 25 years as a psychotherapist I have not found so much as a single exception to this generalization. This kind of temporal covariation was the essential evidential base from which Freud started, and I suggest that if sufficient protocols were available for study, it is the kind of thing which could be subjected to simple statistical test. Since there is no obvious phenotypic overlap in the content, a successful prediction along these lines would strongly corroborate one component of psychoanalytic theory, namely that concerning the urethral cluster. Now I believe that there are many such clusterings which could in principle be subjected to statistical tests, and my expectation is that, if performed, they would provide rather dramatic support for many of Freud's first-level inferences, and pretty clear refutation of others.

Whether or not one is a convinced "Bayesian" is largely irrelevant here, provided we can set *some* safe empirical bounds on the priors, which we can presumably do for the "expectedness" (of our test observation) in the denominator of Bayes's formula, relying on statistics from a large batch of unselected interviews. Even expectedness values = ½ can become a basis for fairly strong corroborators if there are several all "going the right direction." And if we *are* real, feisty, honest-to-goodness "Bayesian personalists" as to probability, it might be plausibly argued that a fair basis for assigning the priors would be guesstimates by academic psychologists largely ignorant of Freud. This basis of prior-probability assignments permits us to go outside the analytic session into those diverse contexts (for which explicit statistics are lacking) of daily life, history, biography, mythology, news media, personal documents, etc.–sources of data which collectively played a major role in convincing the nontherapist intelligentsia that Freud "must have something." Example: No philosophically educated Freudian would have trouble guessing which of these four philosophers wrote a little-known treatise on *wind:* Kant? Locke? Hume? Santayana? A Freudian would call to mind Kant's definition of a moral act as one done *solely* from a sense of duty (rather than, say, a spontaneous loving impulse or a desire to give pleasure); the pedantic punctuality of his daily walk, by which the Königsberg housewives allegedly set their clocks; his remarkable statement that "there can be nothing more dreadful than that the actions of a man should be subject to the will of another"; and his stubborn refusal over many years to speak with a sister following a minor quarrel. But I doubt that a panel of (otherwise knowledgeable) psychologists, ignorant of Freudian theory, would tend to identify Kant as having a scholarly interest in wind–even if we helped them out by adding the fact of Kant's excessive concern with constipation in his later years. The same thing would no doubt be true of my rash prediction (upon first descending the stairs inside the Washington monument) that the wall plaques would show more financial contributions by fire departments than by police departments. (They do.) Point: The very "absurdity" or "far-fetched" character of many psychoanalytic *connections* can be turned to research advantage, because the prior probabilities of such and such correlations among observables are so very differently estimated by one thinking outside the Freudian frame.

As must be apparent from even these brief and (unavoidably) dogmatic remarks, I locate the methodological difficulties of testing psychoanalytic theory differently from many–perhaps most?–who have discussed it, whether as protagonists or critics. For example, I do not waste time defending (as did, say, Frenkel-Brunswik) the introduction of unobservable theoretical entities, knowing as I do that the behaviorist dogma "Science deals only with observables" is historically incorrect and philosophically ludicrous. The *proper* form of the "behavioristic" objection is, as always in sophisticated circles, to the *kind* of theoretical entity being invoked (read: its role in the postulated nomological network, including linkages to data statements). Methodological insight quickly shifts our attention away from such philosophical issues to examination "of the merits," as the lawyers would say. Let me emphasize that I do not rely tendentiously upon philosophy-of-science considerations as a *defense* of psychoanalytic theory either. To rebut a dumb objection is merely to rebut a dumb objection; it does not make a scientific case. Those of us who are betting on a respectable degree of verisimilitude in the Freudian corpus must beware of taking substantive comfort in this indirect way, as some "Chomskyites" are currently taking comfort from (easy) refutations of unsound philosophical positions employed by certain of their S-R-reinforcement opponents. We must try to be honest with ourselves even though we are (as always in science) "betting on a horse race." It simply will not do to get relaxed about the dubious methodological status of, say, a postulated "bargain between ego and superego" as explaining why Smith cuts himself shaving before visiting his mistress, on the ground that the superego is a theoretical construct, and that's peachy, since physicists can't see the neutrino either!

Having mentioned the neutrino, I am led to a comment on falsifiability in the inexact sciences. You may recall that when Pauli cooked up the neutrino idea in 1931—solely to preserve the laws of conservation *ad hoc!*—the theory itself showed that the neutrino hypothesis was probably not falsifiable, because the imagined new particle had zero charge and zero rest mass. It was not until 1956, 25 years later, that a very expensive, never-replicated experiment by Reines and Cowan successfully detected the neutrino (more) "directly." The auxiliary assumptions involved (e.g., would cross section of cadmium nucleus be large enough?) were themselves *so* problematic that a negative experimental result could just as plausibly have counted against *them* as against the theory of interest. While Popper's stress on falsifiability (and the correlative idea that theories become well-corroborated by passing stringent tests) is much needed by the psychologist, partly as an antidote to the current overreliance on mere null-hypothesis refutation as corroborating complex theories (see Rozeboom, 1960; Bakan, 1966; Meehl, 1967; Lykken, 1968), it has become increasingly clear that a too strict and quick application of *modus tollens* would prevent even "good" theories (i.e., theories having high verisimilitude) from getting a foothold. "All theories are lies, but some are white lies, some gray, and some black." The most we can expect of psychodynamic theories in the foreseeable future is that some of them will turn out to be gray lies. My own predilection is therefore for a neo-Popperian position, such as is represented by Feyerabend (1958a, 1958b, 1962a, 1962b, 1963, 1964, 1965a, 1965b, 1966, 1970a, 1970b), Lakatos (1968, 1970), and Maxwell (in press). But what precisely this methodological position means for the strategy of testing psychoanalytic theory is difficult to discern in the present state of the philosophers' controversy. My own tentative predilection is for stronger theories (Platt, 1964; but see Hafner and Presswood, 1965), such strong theories being subjected to more tolerant empirical tests than Popper or Platt recommend. Discussion of this very complicated issue would take us too far afield, but suffice it to say that I now view the position presented in my 1967 paper as too stringent, although its main point is still, I think, a valid one.

Perhaps the psychologist should first learn Popper's main lesson, including why Popper considers such doctrines as psychoanalysis and Marxism to be nonscientific theories like astrology (because all three are pseudo-"confirmable" but not refutable), and then proceed to soften the Popperian rules a bit. Whether these suggested "softenings" really conflict with a sophisticated falsificationism, or whether Popper himself would consider them objectionable, we need not discuss here (but see the distinction between Popper_0, Popper_1, and Popper_2 in Lakatos, 1970). Specifically, I advocate two "cushionings" of the Popperian falsifiability emphasis:

1. A theory is admissible not only if we know how to test it, but if we know *what else we would need to know* in order to test it.

2. A theory need not be abandoned following an adverse result if there are fairly strong results corroborating it, since this combination of circumstances suggests that either (a) the auxiliary hypotheses and *ceteris paribus* clause of the adverse test were not satisfied, or (b) the theory is false as it stands but possesses respectable verisimilitude (i.e., is a gray lie), or both.

I think that these are sensible methodological recommendations that can be rationally defended within a "neo-Popperian" frame, and they do not appear to me to hinge upon resolution of the very technical issues now in controversy among logicians and historians of science. But I hasten to add that such "softening" of the pure, hard-line *modus tollens* rule must not be accompanied by a theoretical commitment such that we persist indefinitely in what Popper stigmatizes as "Parmenidean apologies," clinging to the cherished doctrine in spite of all adverse evidence (Popper, 1965). *When* Parmenidean apologies are desirable, *which kinds,* and *how long* to persist in them ("theoretical tenacity") are difficult questions, to get the feel of which I recommend a reading of Feyerabend's and Lakatos's contributions cited supra.

One big trouble with the application of neo-Popperian strategies to a theory such as Freud's is that the best case for either Parmenidean apologies or for continuing use of a "gray-lie" theory in the face of strong and accepted falsifiers is the concurrent existence of strong corroborators, and this usually (not always) requires that the theory have made successful *point* predictions (i.e., predictions of antecedently improbable numerical values). The successful prediction of a mere directional difference is not of this kind, having too high a prior expectedness in Bayes's Formula lacking the theory of interest. (If I am right, this atheoretical expectedness in the social and biological sciences approaches 1/2 as the power of our significance test increases [Meehl, 1967]). Yet an attempt to formulate psychoanalytic theory so as to generate such high-risk numerical point predictions is hardly feasible at present. For one thing, the auxiliary hypotheses which are normally treated as (relatively) unproblematic in designing a test experiment are unavailable pending the development of powerful, well-corroborated *non*psychodynamic theory (e.g., psycholinguistics). I must say that this state of affairs renders the prospects for cooking up strong tests rather gloomy.

From the standpoint of the experimental psychologist, for whom the experiment (in a fairly tough, restrictive usage of that term) is the ideal method of corroborating or discorroborating theories, the obvious drawbacks of the psychoanalytic hour as a source of data are two, one on the "input" (= control) side and the other on the "output" (= observation) side. On the input side, unless the analyst's enforcement of the Fundamental Rule relies entirely upon the psychological pressure of a silence—a technical maneuver which is sometimes the method of choice but at other times, I think, is clearly not—we have the problem of the timing and content of the analyst's interventions as being themselves "biased" by his theoretical predilections. (It would be interesting to play around with the psychoanalytic analogue to a yoked-box situation in operant-behavior research). On the output side, the problem of "objectifying" the classification of the patient's verbal behavior is so complex that when you begin to think hard about it the most natural response is to throw up your hands in despair. Tentatively, I suggest two contrasting methods of such objectification, to wit: First, we rely upon some standard source such as Roget's *Thesaurus* or the Jenkins-Palermo tables, or a (to-be-constructed) gigantic atlas of couch outputs emitted under "standard" conditions of Fundamental Rule + analyst silence, for determining whether certain words or phrases are thematically or formally linked to others. Such a "scoring system" bypasses the skilled clinical judge and therefore avoids theoretical infection of the data basis. I need hardly point out its grave defect—so grave that a negative result would not be a strong falsifier—which is that the mainly idiographic theme indicators (those which make psychoanalytic therapy fun!) would be lost.

Alternatively, we permit the judgment of a skilled clinician to play a part in classifying the responses, but we systematically prevent his having access to other portions of the material (e.g., to the manifest content of the dream with which the patient began a session) so that he will not be "contaminated" by this material. Point: As much as any area of research in clinical psychology, the study of the psychoanalytic interview brings home the importance of solving, by ingenious methods, the perennial problem of "How do we get the advantages of having a skilled observer, who knows what to listen for and how to classify it, without having the methodological disadvantage that anyone who is skilled in this way has been theoretically brainwashed in the course of his training?" In my view, this is *the* methodological problem in psychoanalytic research.

This brings me to my final point, which is in the nature of a warning prophecy more than a reaction to anything at present happening in psychoanalytic research. The philosophical and historical criticisms against classical positivism and naïve operationism have (quite properly) included emphasis upon the role of theory in determining what, when, and how we observe. But most of the discussion of these matters has drawn its historical examples from astronomy, physics, and chemistry. In these examples, as I read the record, what the experimenter *relied* on in "making observations" was (relatively) nonproblematic and independently corroborated portions of the theoretical network for, say, constructing apparatus. The theory of interest was not "relied on" in that sense, although of course in another sense it was "relied on" in deciding what to do and what to look for. It seems to me important to distinguish these two sorts of reliance on theory, and if they are conflated under the broad statement "Theory determines what we observe," I think confusion results. Furthermore, it is misleading (for several reasons) to equate a mass spectrometer or a piece of litmus paper with a psychotherapist as "instrument of observation." I seem to discern in some quarters of psychology a growing obscurantist tendency–partly antiempirical but also at times even antirational–which relies upon the valuable and insightful writings of Kuhn (1962) and Polanyi (1958) for what I can only characterize as nefarious purposes. It would be unfortunate indeed if efforts to objectify psychoanalytic evidence and inference were abandoned or watered down because of a comfortable reliance on such generalizations as "Scientists have commitments," "We often must stick to a theory for want of a better," "You have to know what you are looking for in order to observe fruitfully," "There is no such thing as a pure observational datum, utterly uninfluenced by one's frame of reference." These are all true and important statements, although the last one needs careful explication and limitation. I do not think general comments of this nature are very helpful in deciding how much an analyst subtly shapes the analysand's discourse by the timing of his interventions ("uncontrolled input"), or whether he classifies a bit of speech as "anal" in a theoretically dogmatic manner ("observer bias in recording output"). If the exciting developments in contemporary philosophy of science are tendentiously employed for obscurantist purposes, to avoid answering perfectly sensible and legitimate criticisms, it will be most unfortunate. The good old positivist questions–"What do you mean?"; "How do you know?"–are still very much in order, and cannot be ruled out of order by historical findings about where Einstein got his ideas. "Millikan relied upon a lot of physical theory, treated as unproblematic, when he 'observed' the charge on the electron" is a correct statement of the case. But such a statement is not, most emphatically *not*, on all fours with "Blauberman [Ross, 1961] is a qualified psychoanalyst, therefore we can rely upon his use of psychoanalytic theory when he classifies a patient's discourse as phallic-intrusive." What one *observes* in the psychoanalytic session is words, postures, gestures, intonation; everything else is inferred. I think the "lowest-level" inferences should be the main object of study for the time being–we should be objectifying and quantifying "low-level theoretical" statements like "Patient is currently anxious, and the thematic content is hostile toward his therapist," rather than highly theoretical statements like "He has superego lacunae" or "His dammed-up libido is flowing back to anal channels." In the process of such objectifying and quantifying research, I can think of no better methodological prescription than the one with which Aristotle set the standards of conceptual rigor as he began his consideration of ethics: "It is the mark of an educated man to look for precision in each class of things just so far as the nature of the subject admits." No more–but no less, either.

REFERENCES

Alexander, F., & Menninger, W. C. (1936), The Relation of Persecutory Delusions to the Functioning of the Gastro-intestinal Tract. *J. Nerv. Ment. Dis.*, 89:541–554. Also in *Studies in Psychosomatic Medicine*, ed. F. Alexander & T. M. French. New York: Ronald Press, 1948, pp. 192–205.

Allers, R., & Teler, J. (1924), On the Utilization of Unnoticed Impressions in Associations. *Psychol. Issues*, Monogr. 7:121–150. New York: International Universities Press, 1960.

Arlow, J. (1969), Unconscious Fantasy and Disturbances of Conscious Experience. *Psychoanal. Quart.*, 38:1–27.

Bakan, D. (1966), The Test of Significance in Psychological Research. *Psychol. Bull.*, 66:423–437.

Beach, F. A., & Jaynes, J. (1954), Effects of Early Experience upon the Behavior of Animals. *Psychol. Bull.*, 51:239–263.

Beech, H. R. (1959), An Experimental Investigation of Sexual Symbolism in Anorexia Nervosa. *Psychosomat. Med.*, 21:277–280.

Benjamin, J. D. (1950), Methodological Considerations in the Validation and Elaboration of Psychoanalytic Personality Theory. *Amer. J. Orthopsychiat.*, 20:139–156.

Beres, D. (1962), The Unconscious Fantasy. *Psychoanal. Quart.*, 31:309–328.

Bevan, W. (1964), Subliminal Stimulation: A Pervasive Problem for Psychology. *Psychol. Bull.*, 61:81–99.

Blum, G. (1949), A Study of the Psychoanalytic Theory of Psychosexual Development. *Genet. Psychol. Monogr.*, 39:3–99.

Brenman, M. (1949), Dreams and Hypnosis. *Psychoanal. Quart.*, 18:455–465.

Bunge, M., ed. (1964), *The Critical Approach: Essays in Honor of Karl R. Popper.* New York: Free Press of Glencoe.

Cofer, C. (1962), Classification of Effects of Modifiers on Discrete Free Associations Made to Verbal Compounds. Technical Report No. 8, Contract NONR 285 (47), Office of Naval Research.

Colby, K. M. (1960), *An Introduction to Psychoanalytic Research.* New York: Basic Books.

Cronbach, L. J., & Meehl, P. E. (1955), Construct Validity in Psychological Tests. *Psychol. Bull.*, 52:281–302.

Dahl, H. (1972), A Quantitative Study of a Psychoanalysis. *Psychoanalysis and Contemporary Science,* 1:237–257. New York: Macmillan.

Dixon, N. F. (1971), *Subliminal Perception: The Nature of a Controversy.* London: McGraw-Hill.

Donchin, E., & Lindsley, D. B., eds. (1969), *Average Evoked Potentials—Methods, Results, Evaluations.* NASA SP 191, Washington, D. C., pp. 199–236.

Engel, G., & Schmale, A. (1967), Psychoanalytic Theory of Somatic Disorder: Conversion, Specificity, and the Disease Onset Situation. *J. Amer. Psychoanal. Assn.,* 15:344–356.

Erickson, M. (1939), Experimental Demonstrations of the Psychopathology of Everyday Life. *Psychoanal. Quart.,* 8:338–353.

Eriksen, C. W. (1960), Discrimination and Learning without Awareness: A Methodological Survey and Evaluation. *Psychol. Rev.,* 67:279–300.

Erikson, E. H. (1954), The Dream Specimen of Psychoanalysis. *J. Amer. Psychoanal. Assn.,* 2:5–56.

Escalona, S. K. (1952), Earliest Phases of Personality Development: A Research Report. *Child Res. Monogr.,* 17(54).

______ (1968), *The Roots of Individuality: Normal Patterns of Development in Infancy.* Chicago: Aldine.

Feyerabend, P. K. (1958a), Attempt at a Realistic Interpretation of Experience. *Proc. Aristot. Soc.,* 58:143–170.

______ (1958b), On the Interpretation of Scientific Theories. *Proceedings of the Twelfth International Congress of Philosophy,* 5:151–159. Venice and Padua.

______ (1962a), Explanation, Reduction, and Empiricism. In *Minnesota Studies in Philosophy of Science,* Vol. 3, ed. H. Feigl & G. Maxwell. Minneapolis: University of Minnesota Press, pp. 28–97.

______ (1962b), Problems of Microphysics. In *Frontiers of Science and Philosophy,* ed. R. G. Colodny. Pittsburgh: University of Pittsburgh Press, pp. 189–283.

______ (1963), How to Be a Good Empiricist—A Plea for Tolerance in Matters Epistemological. In *Delaware Seminar in Philosophy of Science,* Vol. 2, ed. B. Baumrin. New York: Interscience, pp. 3–39.

______ (1964), Realism and Instrumentalism: Comments on the Logic of Factual Support. In *The Critical Approach: Essays in Honor of Karl R. Popper,* ed. M. Bunge. New York: Free Press of Glencoe, pp. 280–308.

______ (1965a), Problems of Empiricism. In *Beyond the Edge of Certainty,* ed. R. G. Colodny. Englewood Cliffs, N. J.: Prentice-Hall, pp. 145–260.

______ (1965b), Reply to Criticism. In *Boston Studies in Philosophy of Science,* Vol. 2, ed. R. S. Cohen & M. W. Wartofsky. New York: Humanities Press, pp. 223–261.

______ (1966), Review [of Nagel's *Structure of Science*]. *Brit. J. Phil. Sci.,* 17:237–249.

______ (1970a), Against Method: Outline of an Anarchistic Theory of Knowledge. In *Minnesota Studies in Philosophy of Science,* Vol. 4, ed. M. Radner & S. Winokur. Minneapolis: University of Minnesota Press, pp. 17–130.

______ (1970b), Problems of Empiricism, Part II. In *The Nature and Function of Scientific Theory,* ed. R. G. Colodny. Pittsburgh: University of Pittsburgh Press, pp. 275–353.

Fisher, C. (1954), Dreams and Perception: The Role of Preconscious and Primary Modes of Perception in Dream Formation. *J. Amer. Psychoanal. Assn.,* 2:389–445.

______ (1956), Dreams, Images, and Perception: A Study of Unconscious-Preconscious Relationships. *J. Amer. Psychoanal. Assn.,* 4:5–48.

______ (1960), Introduction to Preconscious Stimulation in Dreams, Associations, and Images. *Psychol. Issues,* Monogr. 7:1-40. New York: International Universities Press.

______(1965), Psychoanalytic Implications of Recent Research on Sleep and Dreaming. *J. Amer. Psychoanal. Assn.,* 13:197-303.

______& Paul, I. H. (1959), The Effect of Subliminal Visual Stimulation on Images and Dreams: A Validation Study. *J. Amer. Psychoanal. Assn.,* 7:35-83.

Fiss, H., Klein, G. S., & Bokert, E. (1966), Waking Fantasies following Interruption of Two Types of Sleep. *Arch. Gen. Psychiat.,* 14:543-551.

Fraiberg, S., & Freedman, D. A. (1964), Studies in the Ego Development of the Congenitally Blind Child. *The Psychoanalytic Study of the Child,* 19:113-169. New York: International Universities Press.

______Siegal, B. L., & Gibson, R. (1966), The Role of Sound in the Search Behavior of a Blind Infant. *The Psychoanalytic Study of the Child,* 21:327-357. New York: International Universities Press.

Freud, A. (1959), Clinical Studies in Psychoanalysis: Research Project of the Hampstead Child-Therapy Clinic. *The Psychoanalytic Study of the Child,* 14:122-131. New York: International Universities Press.

Freud, S. (1894), The Neuro-Psychoses of Defence. *Standard Edition,* 3:43-68. London: Hogarth Press, 1962.

______(1895), Project for a Scientific Psychology. *Standard Edition,* 1:295-343. London: Hogarth Press, 1966.

______(1896), Further Remarks on the Neuro-Psychoses of Defence. *Standard Edition,* 3:162-185. London: Hogarth Press, 1962.

______(1900), The Interpretation of Dreams. *Standard Edition,* 4 & 5. London: Hogarth Press, 1953.

______(1901), The Psychopathology of Everyday Life. *Standard Edition,* 6. London: Hogarth Press, 1960.

______(1911), Formulations on the Two Principles of Mental Functioning. *Standard Edition,* 12:218-226. London: Hogarth Press, 1958.

______(1914), On Narcissism: An Introduction. *Standard Edition,* 14:73-102. London: Hogarth Press, 1957.

______(1915a), Instincts and Their Vicissitudes. *Standard Edition,* 14:117-140. London: Hogarth Press, 1957.

______(1915b), The Unconscious. *Standard Edition,* 14:166-215. London: Hogarth Press, 1957.

______(1915c), Repression. *Standard Edition,* 14:146-158. London: Hogarth Press, 1957.

______(1917), Mourning and Melancholia. *Standard Edition,* 14:243-258. London: Hogarth Press, 1957.

______(1920), Beyond the Pleasure Principle. *Standard Edition,* 18:7-64. London: Hogarth Press, 1953.

______(1923a), The Ego and the Id. *Standard Edition,* 19:12-66. London: Hogarth Press, 1961.

______(1923b), Two Encyclopaedia Articles: (A) Psycho-Analysis. *Standard Edition,* 18:235-254. London: Hogarth Press, 1955.

______(1925a), Negation. *Standard Edition,* 19:235-239. London: Hogarth Press, 1961.

______(1925b), A Note upon the 'Mystic Writing-Pad.' *Standard Edition,* 19:227-232. London: Hogarth Press, 1961.

——— (1926), Inhibitions, Symptoms and Anxiety. *Standard Edition,* 20:87–172. London: Hogarth Press, 1959.

Gardner, R. W. (1964), The Menninger Foundation Study of Twins and Their Parents. Paper presented at the meeting of the American Psychological Association, September 9.

Gill, M. M. (1963), Topography and Systems in Psychoanalytic Theory. *Psychol. Issues,* Monogr. 10. New York: International Universities Press.

——— (1967), The Primary Process. In Motives and Thought: Psychoanalytic Essays in Honor of David Rapaport, ed. R. R. Holt. *Psychol. Issues,* Monogr. 18/19:260–298. New York: International Universities Press.

——— & Brenman, M. (1959), *Hypnosis and Related States.* New York: International Universities Press.

——— Simon, J., Fink, G., Endicott, N. A., & Paul, I. H. (1968), Studies in Audio-recorded Psychoanalysis: General Considerations. *J. Amer. Psychoanal. Assn.,* 16:230–244.

Goldiamond, I. (1958), Indicators of Perception: I. Subliminal Perception, Subception, Unconscious Perception: An Analysis in Terms of Psychophysical Indicator Methodology. *Psychol. Bull.,* 55:373–411.

——— (1962), Perception. In *Experimental Foundations of Clinical Psychology,* ed. A. J. Bachrach. New York: Basic Books, pp. 280–340.

Goldman, F. (1948), Breast Feeding and Character Formation. *J. Pers.,* 17:83–103.

Hafner, E. M., & Presswood, S. (1965), Strong Inference and Weak Interactions. *Science,* 149:503–510.

Haider, M., Spong, P., & Lindsley, D. B. (1964), Attention, Vigilance, and Cortical Evoked-Potentials in Humans. *Science,* 145:180–182.

Hernández-Peón, R., Scherrer, H., & Jouvet, M. (1956), Modification of Electric Activity in Cochlear Nucleus during "Attention" in Unanesthetized Cats. *Science,* 123:331–332.

Hilgard, E. R. (1952), Experimental Approaches to Psychoanalysis. In *Psychoanalysis as Science,* ed. E. Pumpian-Mindlin. Stanford: Stanford University Press, pp. 3–45.

Holt, R. R. (1967), The Development of the Primary Process: A Structural View. In Motives and Thought: Psychoanalytic Essays in Honor of David Rapaport. *Psychol. Issues,* Monogr. 18/19:345–383. New York: International Universities Press.

——— & Havel, J. (1960), A Method for Assessing Primary and Secondary Process in the Rorschach. In *Rorschach Psychology,* ed. M. Rickers-Ovsiankina. New York: Wiley, pp. 263–315.

Hunt, J. McV. (1941), The Effects of Infant Feeding-Frustration upon Adult Hoarding in the Albino Rat. *J. Abnorm. Soc. Psychol.,* 36:338–360.

Jaffe, J. (1963), Electronic Computers in Psychoanalytic Research. In *Science and Psychoanalysis,* Vol. 6, ed. J. H. Masserman. New York: Grune and Stratton.

Kamiya, J. (1964), Conditioned Introspection: Humans Can Learn to Detect and Control Their EEG Alpha Rhythms. Paper presented at the meeting of the Society for Psychophysiological Research, Washington, D. C., October.

Kaplan, A. (1964), *The Conduct of Inquiry.* San Francisco: Chandler.

Keet, C. D. (1948), Two Verbal Techniques in a Miniature Counseling Situation. *Psychol. Monogr.,* 62(7, Whole No. 294).

Kernberg, O. F., Burstein, E. D., Coyne, L., Appelbaum, A., Horwitz, L., & Voth, H. (1972), Psychotherapy and Psychoanalysis: Final Report of the Menninger Foundation's Psychotherapy Research Project. *Bull. Menninger Clin.*, 36:3–275.

Klein, G. S. (1959), Consciousness in Psychoanalytic Theory: Some Implications for Current Research in Perception. *J. Amer. Psychoanal. Assn.*, 7:5–34.

______ (1967), Peremptory Ideation: Structure and Force in Motivated Ideas. In Motives and Thought: Psychoanalytic Essays in Honor of David Rapaport, ed. R. R. Holt. *Psychol. Issues,* Monogr. 18/19:80–130. New York: International Universities Press.

Kohut, H. (1964), Some Problems of a Metapsychological Formulation of Fantasy. *Int. J. Psycho-Anal.*, 45:199–202.

Kubie, L. S. (1952), Problems and Techniques of Psychoanalytic Validation and Progress. In *Psychoanalysis as Science,* ed. E. Pumpian-Mindlin. Stanford: Stanford University Press, pp. 46–124.

Kuhn, T. S. (1962), *The Structure of Scientific Revolutions.* Chicago: University of Chicago Press.

Lakatos, I. (1968), Changes in the Problem of Inductive Logic. In *The Problem of Inductive Logic,* ed. I. Lakatos. Amsterdam: North-Holland Publishing Co., pp. 315–417.

______ (1970), Falsification and the Methodology of Scientific Research Programmes. In *Criticism and the Growth of Knowledge,* ed. I. Lakatos & A. Musgrave. Cambridge: Cambridge University Press, pp. 91–95.

Levy, D. M. (1934), Experiments on the Sucking Reflex and Social Behavior of Dogs. *Amer. J. Orthopsychiat.*, 4:203–224.

______ (1952), Animal Psychology in Its Relation to Psychiatry. In *Dynamic Psychology,* ed. F. Alexander & H. Ross. Chicago: University of Chicago Press, pp. 483–507.

Libet, B., Alberts, W. W., Wright, E. W., Jr., & Feinstein, B. (1967), Responses of Human Somatosensory Cortex to Stimuli below Threshold for Conscious Sensation. *Science*, 158:1597–1600.

Luborsky, L. (1953), Intraindividual Repetitive Measurements (P Technique) in Understanding Psychotherapeutic Change. In *Psychotherapy: Theory and Research,* ed. O. H. Mowrer. New York: Ronald Press, pp. 389–413.

______ (1964), A Psychoanalytic Research on Momentary Forgetting during Free Association. *Bull. Philadelphia Assn. Psychoanal.*, 14:119–137.

______ (1966), A Cognitive Disturbance Measure for Speech Samples: A Scoring Manual and Validity Studies. Mimeographed.

______ (1967), Momentary Forgetting during Psychotherapy and Psychoanalysis: A Theory and Research Method. In Motives and Thought: Psychoanalytic Essays in Honor of David Rapaport, ed. R. R. Holt. *Psychol. Issues,* Monogr. 18/19:177–217. New York: International Universities Press.

______ (1970), New Directions in Research on Neurotic and Psychosomatic Symptoms. *Amer. Scient.*, 58:661–668.

______ & Auerbach, A. H. (1969), The Symptom-Context Method: Quantitative Studies of Symptom Formation in Psychotherapy. *J. Amer. Psychoanal. Assn.*, 17:68–99.

______ Graff, H., Pulver, S., & Curtis, H. (in press), A Clinical-Quantitative Examination of Consensus on the Concept of Transference. *Arch. Gen. Psychiat.*

——— & Mintz, J. (in press), Onset Conditions for Momentary Forgetting during Psychoanalysis: Explorations of Controlled Methods of Observation. *Psychoanalysis and Contemporary Science,* Vol. 3. New York: Macmillan.

——— & Shevrin, H. (1956), Dreams and Day Residues: A Study of the Poetzl Observation. *Bull. Menninger Clin.*, 20:135–148.

——— ——— (1962), Artificial Induction of Day-Residues—An Illustration and an Examination. *Bull. Philadelphia Assn. Psychoanal.*, 12:149–167.

Lykken, D. T. (1968), Statistical Significance in Psychological Research. *Psychol. Bull.*, 70:151–159.

Madison, P. (1956), Freud's Repression Concept: A Survey and Attempted Clarification. *Int. J. Psycho-Anal.*, 37:75–81.

Mahl, G. (1956), Disturbances and Silences in the Patient's Speech in Psychotherapy. *J. Abnorm. Soc. Psychol.*, 53:1–15.

Malamud, W., & Lindner, F. E. (1931), Dreams and Their Relationship to Recent Impressions. *Arch. Neurol. Psychiat.*, 25:1080–1099.

Maxwell, G. (in press), Corroboration with Demarcation. In *The Philosophy of Karl Popper,* ed. P. A. Schilpp. Lasalle: Open Court.

Meehl, P. E. (1967), Theory-Testing in Psychology and Physics: A Methodological Paradox. *Phil. Sci.*, 34:103–115.

Miller, N. E. (1948), Theory and Experiment relating Psychoanalytic Displacement to Stimulus-Response Generalization. *J. Abnorm. Soc. Psychol.,* 43:155–178.

Nachmansohn, M. (1925), Concerning Experimentally Produced Dreams. In *Organization and Pathology of Thought,* ed. D. Rapaport. New York: Columbia University Press, 1951, pp. 257–287.

Nagera, H., et al. (1969), *The Hampstead Clinic Psychoanalytic Library,* Vols. 1–7. New York: Basic Books.

Oppenheimer, R. (1956), Analogy in Science. *Amer. Psychol.*, 11:127–135.

Pap, A. (1953), Reduction Sentences and Open Concepts. *Methodos,* 5:3–30.

——— (1958), *Semantics and Necessary Truth.* New Haven: Yale University Press.

Perky, C. W. (1910), An Experimental Study of Imagination. *Amer. J. Psychol.*, 21:422–452.

Pine, F. (1964), The Bearing of Psychoanalytic Theory on Selected Issues in Research on Marginal Stimulation. *J. Nerv. Ment. Dis.*, 138:205–222.

Platt, J. R. (1964), Strong Inference. *Science,* 146:347–353.

Polanyi, M. (1958), *Personal Knowledge.* London: Routledge and Kegan Paul.

Popper, K. R. (1959), *The Logic of Scientific Discovery.* New York: Basic Books.

——— (1962), *Conjectures and Refutations.* New York: Basic Books.

——— (1965), Rationality and the Search for Invariants. Paper presented at the International Colloquium on Philosophy of Science, July.

Pötzl, O. (1917), The Relationship between Experimentally Induced Dream Images and Indirect Vision. *Psychol. Issues,* Monogr. 7:41–120. New York: International Universities Press, 1960.

Pribram, H. H., Spinelli, D. N., & Kamback, M. C. (1967), Electrocortical Correlates of Stimulus Response and Reinforcement. *Science,* 157:94–96.

Pumpian-Mindlin, E., ed. (1952), *Psychoanalysis as Science.* Stanford: Stanford University Press.

Rapaport, D. (1942), *Emotions and Memory,* 2nd ed. New York: International Universities Press, 1950.

______ ed. (1951a), *Organization and Pathology of Thought.* New York: Columbia University Press.

______ (1951b), States of Consciousness. *Collected Papers.* New York: Basic Books, 1967, pp. 385–404.

______ (1957), Cognitive Structures. *Collected Papers.* New York: Basic Books, 1967, pp. 631–664.

______ (1959a), The Structure of Psychoanalytic Theory: A Systematizing Attempt. *Psychol. Issues,* Monogr. 6. New York: International Universities Press, 1960.

______ (1959b), The Theory of Attention Cathexis. *Collected Papers.* New York: Basic Books, 1967, pp. 778–794.

Reichenbach, H. (1938), *Experience and Prediction.* Chicago: University of Chicago Press.

Roffenstein, G. (1924), Experiments on Symbolization in Dreams. In *Organization and Pathology of Thought,* ed. D. Rapaport. New York: Columbia University Press, 1951, pp. 249–256.

Rosenwald, G. C. (1972), Effectiveness of Defenses against Anal Impulse Arousal. *J. Consult. Clin. Psychol.,* 39:292–298.

______ Mendelsohn, G. A., Fontana, A., & Portz, A. T. (1966), An Action Test of Hypotheses concerning the Anal Personality. *J. Abnorm. Psychol.,* 71: 304–309.

Rosenzweig, S. (1937), The Experimental Study of Psychoanalytic Concepts. *Charact. & Pers.,* 6:61–71.

______ & Mason, C. (1934), An Experimental Study of Memory in Relation to the Theory of Repression. *Brit. J. Psychol.,* 24:247–265.

Ross, L. (1961), The Ordeal of Doctor Blauberman. *The New Yorker,* May 13:39–48. Also in *Vertical and Horizontal.* New York: Simon and Schuster, 1963.

Rozeboom, W. (1960), The Fallacy of the Null-Hypothesis Significance Test. *Psychol. Bull.,* 67:416–428.

Sandler, J. (1962a), The Hampstead Index as an Instrument of Psychoanalytic Research. *Int. J. Psycho-Anal.,* 43:287–291.

______ (1962b), The Classification of Superego Material in the Hampstead Index. *The Psychoanalytic Study of the Child,* 17:107–127. New York: International Universities Press.

______ & Nagera, H. (1963), Aspects of the Metapsychology of Fantasy. *The Psychoanalytic Study of the Child,* 18:159–194. New York: International Universities Press.

Scheerer, M. (1945–1946), Problems of Performance Analysis in the Study of Personality. *Ann. N. Y. Acad. Sci.,* 46:653–678.

Schlesinger, H. (1964), The Place of Forgetting in Memory Functioning. Paper presented at the meeting of the American Psychoanalytic Association, New York, December.

Schlesinger, V. G. (1963), Anal Personality Traits and Occupational Choice: A Study of Accountants, Chemical Engineers and Educational Psychologists. Unpublished doctoral dissertation, University of Michigan.

Schmidt, E., & Brown, P. (1965), Experimental Testing of Two Psychoanalytic Hypotheses. *Brit. J. Med. Psychol.,* 38:177–180.

Schrötter, K. (1911), Experimental Dreams. In *Organization and Pathology of Thought,* ed. D. Rapaport. New York: Columbia University Press, 1951, pp. 234-248.

Sears, R. R. (1943), *Survey of Objective Studies of Psychoanalytic Concepts.* Social Science Research Council, Bulletin No. 51.

______ (1944), Experimental Analysis of Psychoanalytic Phenomena. In *Personality and the Behavior Disorders,* Vol. 1, ed. J. McV. Hunt. New York: Ronald Press, pp. 306-332.

Shakow, D. (1960), The Recorded Psychoanalytic Interview as an Objective Approach to Research in Psychoanalysis. *Psychoanal. Quart.,* 29:82-97.

Shevrin, H. (1968), Perception, Registration, and Normal Inhibition. Paper presented at the meeting of the Rapaport Study Group, Stockbridge, Massachusetts, June.

______ & Fisher, C. (1967), Changes in the Effects of a Waking Subliminal Stimulus as a Function of Dreaming and Nondreaming Sleep. *J. Abnorm. Psychol.,* 72:362-368.

______ & Fritzler, D. E. (1968a), Visual Evoked Response Correlates of Unconscious Mental Processes. *Science,* 161:295-298.

______ ______ (1968b), Brain Response Correlates of Repressiveness. *Psychol. Rep.,* 23:887-892.

______ & Luborsky, L. (1958), The Measurement of Preconscious Perception in Dreams and Images: An Investigation of the Poetzl Phenomenon. *J. Abnorm. Soc. Psychol.,* 56:285-294.

______ ______ (1961), The Rebus Technique: A Method for Studying Primary-Process Transformations of Briefly Exposed Pictures. *J. Nerv. Ment. Dis.,* 133:479-488.

______ & Rennick, P. (1967), Cortical Response to a Tactile Stimulus during Attention, Mental Arithmetic and Free Associations. *Psychophysiol.,* 3:381-388.

______ Smith, W. H., & Fritzler, D. E. (1969), Repressiveness as a Factor in the Subliminal Activation of Brain and Verbal Responses. *J. Nerv. Ment. Dis.,* 149:261-269.

______ ______ ______ (1970), Subliminally Stimulated Brain and Verbal Responses of Twins Differing in Repressiveness. *J. Abnorm. Psychol.,* 76:39-46.

______ ______ ______ (1971), Average Evoked Response and Verbal Correlates of Unconscious Mental Processes. *Psychophysiol.,* 8:149-162.

Shipley, T. E., & Veroff, J. (1952), A Projective Measure of Need for Affiliation. *J. Exper. Psychol.,* 43:349-356.

Silberer, H. (1909), Report on a Method of Eliciting and Observing Certain Symbolic Hallucination-Phenomena. In *Organization and Pathology of Thought,* ed. D. Rapaport. New York: Columbia University Press, 1951, pp. 195-207.

Simon, J., rep. (1970), Research in Psychoanalysis: Experimental Studies. *J. Amer. Psychoanal. Assn.,* 18:644-654.

Spence, D. P. (1964), Conscious and Preconscious Influences on Recall: Another Example of the Restricting Effects of Awareness. *J. Abnorm. Soc. Psychol.,* 68:92-99.

______ (1969a), PL/1 Programs for Content Analysis. *Behav. Sci.,* 14:432-433.

______ (1969b), Computer Measurement of Process and Content in Psychoanalysis. *Trans. N. Y. Acad. Sci.,* 31:828-841.

_____ & Holland, B. (1962), The Restricting Effects of Awareness: A Paradox and an Explanation. *J. Abnorm. Soc. Psychol.*, 64:163–174.

Spitz, R. (1945), Hospitalism: An Inquiry into the Genesis of Psychiatric Conditions in Early Childhood. *The Psychoanalytic Study of the Child,* 1:53–74. New York: International Universities Press.

_____ (1946), Hospitalism: A Follow-Up Report. *The Psychoanalytic Study of the Child,* 2:113–117. New York: International Universities Press.

_____ & Wolf, K. M. (1946a), The Smiling Response: A Contribution to the Ontogenesis of Social Relationships. *Genet. Psychol. Monogr.*, 34:57–125.

_____ _____ (1946b), Anaclitic Depression: An Inquiry into the Genesis of Psychiatric Conditions in Early Childhood. *The Psychoanalytic Study of the Child,* 2:313–342. New York: International Universities Press.

Stross, L., & Shevrin, H. (1968), Thought Organization in Hypnosis and the Waking State. *J. Nerv. Ment. Dis.*, 147:272–288.

Symposium on Fantasy (1964), *Int. J. Psycho-Anal.*, 45:171–201.

Tecce, J. J. (1970), Attention and Evoked Potentials in Man. In *Attention: Contemporary Theory and Analysis,* ed. D. I. Mostofsky. New York: Appleton-Century-Crofts.

Thorndike, E. L., & Lorge, I. (1944), *The Teacher's Word Book of 30,000 Words.* New York: Teachers College, Columbia University Bureau of Publications.

Varendonck, J. (1921), *The Psychology of Daydreams.* New York: Macmillan.

Wallerstein, R. S., et al. (1956), The Psychotherapy Research Project of the Menninger Foundation. *Bull. Menninger Clin.*, 2:221–278.

Wilson, F. (1967), Definition and Discovery: I, II. *Brit. J. Phil. Sci.*, 18:287–303; 19:43–56.

_____ (1968), Is Operationism Unjust to Temperature? *Synthese,* 18:394–422.

Winer, B. J. (1962), *Statistical Principles in Experimental Design.* New York: McGraw-Hill.

Wolff, P. H. (1963), Observations on the Early Development of Smiling. In *Determinants of Infant Behavior,* Vo. 2, ed. B. M. Foss. New York: Wiley.

_____ (1964), The Pertinence of Direct Infant Observation for Psychoanalytic Theory. Paper presented at the meeting of the American Psychoanalytic Association, December.

SUPPLEMENTAL BIBLIOGRAPHY

Bellak, L. (1961), Research in Psychoanalysis. *Psychoanal. Quart.*, 30:519–548.

Brenner, C. (1968), Psychoanalysis and Science. *J. Amer. Psychoanal. Assn.*, 16:675–696.

Edel, A. (1964), The Concept of the Unconscious: Some Analytic Preliminaries. *Phil. Sci.*, 31:18–33.

Ellis, A. (1950), An Introduction to the Principles of Scientific Psychoanalysis. *Genet. Psychol. Monogr.*, 41:147–212.

Escalona, S. (1952), Problems in Psycho-Analytic Research. *Int. J. Psycho-Anal.*, 33:11–21.

Farrell, B. A. (1954), The Scientific Testing of Psychoanalytic Findings and Theory. In *The Study of Personality*, ed. H. Brand. New York: Wiley, pp. 449–457.

Feigl, H., & Scriven, M., eds. (1956), *Minnesota Studies in the Philosophy of Science*, Vol. 1. *The Foundations of Science and the Concepts of Psychology and Psychoanalysis.* Minneapolis: University of Minnesota Press.

Frenkel-Brunswik, E. (1954), The Meaning of Psychoanalytic Concepts and Confirmation of Psychoanalytic Theories. *Sci. Monthly*, 79:293-300.

——— (1959), Psychoanalysis and the Unity of Science. *J. Amer. Psychoanal. Assn.*, 7:127–145.

Glover, E. (1952), Research Methods in Psycho-Analysis. *Int. J. Psycho-Anal.*, 33:403–409.

Greenfield, N., & Lewis, W. C., eds. (1965), *Psychoanalysis and Current Biological Thought.* Madison: University of Wisconsin Press.

Grinker, R. R. (1955), Validation of Psychoanalytic Theory. Summarized by H. W. Brown. *J. Amer. Psychoanal. Assn.*, 3:489–505.

Hilgard, E. R. (1962), The Scientific Status of Psychoanalysis. In *Logic, Methodology, and Philosophy of Science*, ed. E. Nagel, P. Suppes, & A. Tarski. Stanford: Stanford University Press.

Kubie, L. S. (1947), The Fallacious Use of Quantitative Concepts in Dynamic Psychology. *Psychoanal. Quart.*, 16:507–518.

——— (1953), Psychoanalysis as a Basic Science. In *Twenty Years of Psychoanalysis*, ed. F. Alexander & H. Ross. New York: Norton, pp. 120–145.

Luborsky, L., & Spence, D. (1971), Quantitative Research on Psychoanalytic Therapy. In *Handbook of Psychotherapy and Behavior Change*, ed. A. E. Bergin & S. L. Garfield. New York: Wiley, pp. 408–437.

Oken, D. (1965), Operational Research Concepts and Psychoanalytic Theory. In *Psychoanalysis and Current Biological Thought*, ed. N. Greenfield & W. C. Lewis. Madison: University of Wisconsin Press, pp. 181–200.

Richfield, J. (1954), On the Scientific Status of Psychoanalysis. *Sci. Monthly*, 79:306–309.

Rapaport, A. (1967), *Psychoanalysis as Science.* Topeka, Kansas. Unpublished.

Schmidl, F. (1955), The Problem of Scientific Validation in Psycho-Analytic Interpretation. *Int. J. Psycho-Anal.*, 36:105–113.

______ (1959), Psychoanalysis as Science. *J. Amer. Psychoanal. Assn.*, 7:127–145.

Skinner, B. F. (1956), Critique of Psychoanalytic Concepts and Theories. In *Minnesota Studies in the Philosophy of Science*, Vol. 1. *The Foundations of Science and the Concepts of Psychology and Psychoanalysis*, ed. H. Feigl & M. Scriven. Minneapolis: University of Minnesota Press.

Waelder, R. (1962), Review of S. Hook, *Psychoanalysis, Scientific Method, and Philosophy. J. Amer. Psychoanal. Assn.*, 10:617–637.

Wallerstein, R. S., & Simpson, H. (1971), Issues in Research in the Psychoanalytic Process. *Int. J. Psycho-Anal.*, 52:11–50.

Wolman, B. B. (1964), Evidence in Psychoanalytic Research. *J. Amer. Psychoanal. Assn.*, 12:717–733.

INDEX

ABOUT THE EDITOR

MARTIN MAYMAN received his Ph.D. in psychology from the University of Kansas in 1947, after having spent three years studying clinical psychology with David Rapaport at the Menninger Foundation. From 1946 to 1951 he taught in the combined University of Kansas-Menninger Foundation training program in clinical psychology, after which he set up and directed the Menninger Foundation's postdoctoral training program in clinical psychology. He was graduated from the Topeka Institute for Psychoanalysis in 1960 and became a member of its faculty, conducting seminars on the clinical concepts of psychoanalysis and psychoanalytic ego psychology. In 1967 he joined the faculty of the University of Michigan where he teaches in the graduate clinical program. Since 1968 he has been teaching at the Michigan Psychoanalytic Institute. Psychoanalytic ego psychology and its application to the understanding of early memories, dreams, and projective test data has been a guiding influence in all his work. His publications include papers on clinical matters, issues of clinical training, and the psychoanalytic study of personality. He has coauthored, with Karl A. Menninger and Paul Pruyser, two textbooks in psychiatry, *The Vital Balance* and *Manual for Psychiatric Case Study.*

ABOUT THE AUTHORS

CAROL GORDON is a student in the graduate clinical program at New York University, and has completed all requirements for the degree except the dissertation.

PHILIP S. HOLZMAN received his Ph.D. from the University of Kansas in 1952. He was a clinical psychologist at the Menninger Foundation for 22 years, was Director of Research Training at the Menninger Foundation, and a training and supervising psychoanalyst at the Topeka Institute for Psychoanalysis. He is now Professor in the Departments of Psychiatry and Psychology at the University of Chicago, and is a training and supervising psychoanalyst at the Chicago Institute for Psychoanalysis. He has written extensively on his research in cognitive controls, vocal feedback, and the perceptual aspects of schizophrenic disorganization. He is the author of *Psychoanalysis and Psychopathology* and coauthor with Karl Menninger of the revised edition of *The Theory of Psychoanalytic Technique.*

LESTER LUBORSKY received his Ph.D. from Duke University in 1945. After teaching two years at the University of Illinois, he joined the Research Department of the Menninger Foundation in 1947. Since 1959, he has been at the University of Pennsylvania School of Medicine, where he is Professor of Psychology in Psychiatry. He is a graduate of the Topeka Psychoanalytic Institute and was for several years an instructor at the Institute of the Philadelphia Association for Psychoanalysis. He holds a Research Scientist Award from the National Institute of Mental Health and directs the Psychotherapy Research Unit of the Department of Psychiatry of the University of Pennsylvania School of Medicine.

PAUL E. MEEHL received his Ph.D. in clinical psychology in 1945 from the University of Minnesota, where he is at present Regents' Professor of Psychology, Adjunct Professor of Law, Professor in the Psychiatry Research Unit, and Professor in the Minnesota Center for Philosophy of Science. He has coauthored *Modern Learning Theory* and *Atlas for Clinical Interpretation of the MMPI,* and authored *Clinical versus Statistical Prediction* and *Psychodiagnosis: Selected Papers* (in press), as well as numerous articles in psychological, philosophical, and legal journals. His current research and teaching interests include taxonomic statistics, behavior genetics, objectifying personality assessment, philosophical psychology, and forensic psychology. He is a past president of the American Psychological Association, and a recipient of its Distinguished Scientific Contributor Award, as well as of the Distinguished Contributor Prize of Division 12 (Clinical). He engages in a part-time private practice of psychotherapy at the Nicollet Clinic in Minneapolis, where he characterizes his orientation as "one-third psychoanalytic, one-third RET, and one-third Skinnerian."

HOWARD SHEVRIN received his Ph.D. from Cornell University in 1954. After completing a postdoctoral fellowship in clinical psychology at the Menninger Foundation, he joined the Menninger staff in 1954. He is a graduate of the Topeka Institute for Psychoanalysis. In 1973 he became Professor of Psychology and Chief Psychologist in the Department of Psychiatry at the University of Michigan. He divides his time between clinical work and the laboratory, where his research has concerned the nature of unconscious mental processes. Articles describing this and related work have appeared in *Science, Journal of Abnormal Psychology, Psychophysiology, Journal of Nervous and Mental Disease, Psychological Reports,* and elsewhere.

DONALD P. SPENCE received his Ph.D. in clinical psychology from Teachers College, Columbia, in 1955. He is a Professor of Psychology at New York University, and a staff member of the Research Center for Mental Health, New York University. He has recently become an associate research member of the New York Psychoanalytic Institute. He is a coauthor of "Cognitive Control: A Study of Individual Consistencies in Cognitive Behavior," *Psychological Issues,* Monograph No. 4.

PSYCHOLOGICAL ISSUES

No. 1—Erik H. Erikson: *Identity and the Life Cycle; Selected Papers.* Historical Introduction by David Rapaport

No. 2—I. H. Paul: *Studies in Remembering; The Reproduction of Connected and Extended Verbal Material*

No. 3—Fritz Heider: *On Perception, Event Structure, and the Psychological Environment.* Preface by George S. Klein

No. 4—Riley W. Gardner, Philip S. Holzman, George S. Klein, Harriet Linton, and Donald P. Spence: *Cognitive Control; A Study of Individual Consistencies in Cognitive Behavior*

No. 5—Peter H. Wolff: *The Developmental Psychologies of Jean Piaget and Psychoanalysis*

No. 6—David Rapaport: *The Structure of Psychoanalytic Theory; A Systematizing Attempt*

No. 7—Otto Pötzl, Rudolf Allers, and Jakob Teler: *Preconscious Stimulation in Dreams, Associations, and Images; Classical Studies.* Introduction by Charles Fisher

No. 8—Riley W. Gardner, Douglas N. Jackson, and Samuel J. Messick: *Personality Organization in Cognitive Controls and Intellectual Abilities.*

No. 9—Fred Schwartz and Richard O. Rouse: *The Activation and Recovery of Associations*

No. 10—Merton M. Gill: *Topography and Systems in Psychoanalytic Theory*

No. 11—Robert W. White: *Ego and Reality in Psychoanalytic Theory: A Proposal regarding the Independent Ego Energies*

No. 12—Ivo Kohler: *The Formation and Transformation of the Perceptual World.* Introduction by James J. Gibson

No. 13—David Shakow and David Rapaport: *The Influence of Freud on American Psychology*

No. 14—Heinz Hartmann, Ernst Kris, and Rudolph M. Loewenstein: *Papers on Psychoanalytic Psychology*

No. 15—Wolfgang Lederer: *Dragons, Delinquents, and Destiny; An Essay on Positive Superego Functions.* Introduction by Roy Schafer

No. 16—Peter Amacher: *Freud's Neurological Education and Its Influence on Psychoanalytic Theory*

No. 17—Peter H. Wolff: *The Causes, Controls, and Organization of Behavior in the Neonate*

No. 18/19—Robert R. Holt, Ed.: *Motives and Thought; Psychoanalytic Essays in Honor of David Rapaport*

No. 20—John Chynoweth Burnham: *Psychoanalysis and American Medicine, 1894-1918; Medicine, Science, and Culture*

No. 21—Helen D. Sargent, Leonard Horwitz, Robert S. Wallerstein, and Ann Appelbaum: *Prediction in Psychotherapy Research: A Method for the Transformation of Clinical Judgments into Testable Hypotheses*

No. 22—Marjorie Grene, Ed.: *Toward a Unity of Knowledge*

No. 23—Fred Schwartz and Peter H. Schiller: *A Psychoanalytic Model of Attention and Learning*

No. 24—Bernard Landis: *Ego Boundaries*

No. 25/26—Emanuel Peterfreund in collaboration with Jacob T. Schwartz: *Information, Systems, and Psychoanalysis; An Evolutionary Biological Approach to Psychoanalytic Theory*

No. 27—Louis Breger, Ian Hunter, and Ron W. Lane: *The Effect of Stress on Dreams*

No. 28—Edith Levitov Garduk and Ernest A. Haggard: *Immediate Effects on Patients of Psychoanalytic Interpretations*

No. 29—Erich Goldmeier: *Similarity in Visually Perceived Forms.* Foreword by Irvin Rock

PSYCHOLOGICAL ISSUES

MONOGRAPHS IN PREPARATION

ELSE FRENKEL-BRUNSWIK: *Selected Papers,* ed. by N. Heiman and J. Grant

JOSEPH H. D ... uc- tion by

MICHAEL P ...

STANLEY I. ... *i- ables i* ...